THE TO
MU~~R~~D~~E~~R

Anatomy
of
a Victorian Crime
by
SHAUN VILLIERS EVERETT

Published by

Victorian Crime and Punishment Series

ISBN-13: 978-1546383321

First Published in Great Britain in 2017 by George Wombwell Collection

Copyright Shaun Villiers Everett 2017

Shaun Villiers Everett has asserted his right under the Copyright, Design and Patents Act, 1988 to be identified as the author of this work.

Address for the author is
shaunvillierseverett@shaunvillierseverett.com

Dedicated to all those innocent of crime
that have been wrongly incarcerated or have lost their
lives through a miscarriage of justice.

Contents

1 Introduction ii
2. The Crime 3
3 The Inquest 18
4. Changing Victorian Attitude to Capital Punishment 68
5 The Trial 73
6 Conclusions 115
8 After the Trial 124
9 The Fate of Henry Harrington, Innocent Man? 126
Appendix I Census, Parish, Index and other Records 129

1 Introduction

This, the first in a series concerning Victorian Crime and Punishment, is a little-known murder, committed in 1851. Henry Harrington was committed for trial in March 1852 at the Essex Assizes in Chelmsford, Essex. This book sets out the events that took part on that day in November and those that led up to his trial, including the inquest, hastily convened during the week of the murder. The search for evidence and the recording of witness statements is set out as reported by the local and national newspapers of the period.

The location is Tollesbury in rural Essex, a small, but thriving fishing village on the expansive Essex coastal marshes. Tollesbury's main activity in mid-Victorian England, was oyster dredging, and many 'dredgermen', as they were known, were living in the village and the surrounding countryside. It is the events surrounding two dredgermen's' families, the Cobbs and the Wash's, close neighbours, that resulted in the brutal murder of one man's wife during the winter of November 1851 and the subsequent search and bringing to trial her killer.

It is based on facts and reports as well as court documents from the National Archives, Kew, London. In some chapters, it has been dramatized to affect a good read. Where extensive reports exist, they have been accurately reproduced from the original reports. At no time does the text stray from the case, except where explanations are needed to make a point.

2. The Crime

It was the morning of Tuesday, 25th November 1851, and the sun had not yet risen over the distant frosted marshes of this harsh coastal environment. Soon, the sun would light up the November skies as the biting easterly wind forced the grassy banks around the many tidal inlets from the now rising Blackwater River. This was Tollesbury, a thriving and bustling fishing village on this intensely busy river, and it came to life as it did every day at this time, or when the high tide beckoned, year after year.

James Cobb (33), of 97 East Street, Tollesbury, oysterman (or dredgerman), was getting up within his cottage, close to the centre of the village and preparing to go to his work at the village's fine oyster layings, a little way off the main thoroughfare through the village and to the eastern shore of the Blackwater at Tollesbury Fleet[1]. He lived with his wife Elizabeth (33) and their 6-year-old adopted daughter Elisa Spurgin, in one of a row of cottages, approximately 1km from the shore line. He went downstairs leaving his wife to her normal practice of sleeping in for another hour or so. It was about 5.30 am and he would soon be aboard his smack and hard at work[2].

James was well known as an Oyster dredgerman, and a well-respected member of this fishing community in Tollesbury, which by 1851, amounting to over 3000 inhabitants, many brought in by the fishing and surrounding farming industries. They came from all over, it seemed, both mariners and farm labourers from the surrounding Essex villages, arriving to seek their fortunes from the sea. The Oyster industry was so much in demand at that time, that residents had opened their homes up to this new flood of labour. James Cobb,

---

[1] Today we would call these oyster beds. The Fleet was an inlet that reached far inland towards the village.

[2] A Smack is a small fishing boat designed for dredging oysters. Other larger Smacks also trawled their catch, as at Lowestoft on the Suffolk coast.

was born and bred in Tollesbury and to meet the demand for new blood, had opened his home with one William Mason and Edward Pewter, both dredgermen, who now slept in the second upstairs room in this traditional village cottage. Pewter though, had left the house the night before and was therefore not there for breakfast. Mason had already risen, by the time James had come downstairs and had made himself ready for work. James finished his breakfast, put on his work clothes and then returned upstairs, through Mason's room, which he had to pass to get to his and Elizabeth's own bedroom. He bent over and kissed his wife, now awake, and said that he would be back after two o'clock. He heard Mason leave as he went back downstairs and shortly followed his lodger by the only door, soon after six o'clock, leaving it latched with the key inside. He walked briskly down East Street, pulling his hat down over his face to keep out the east wind, that came through East Street towards the village centre.

A little way down the road from Cobb's cottage, Joseph Kiev, a long-time waterman, rose from his bed about half past six o'clock, and left his cottage and started off in the direction of the neighbouring village of Salcot to the north of Tollesbury[3]. By this time, James Cobb was well on his way to the Fleet. Looking up the street, Kiev noticed a man at the end of Cobb's cottage It was about ten minutes to seven and still not yet light, but he noticed that the man was standing against the school yard gate which backed onto Cobb's cottage[4].

When the man arrived at a neighbouring cottage gate, Kiev noticed, he went into its yard. Kiev could not distinguish the features of this man, apart from observing that he had been wearing a cap, the light being not yet strong enough to illuminate his facial features, but he thought that it might be the outline of Henry Harrington, whom he had known since Harrington's childhood, and a lodger at the

---

[3] A waterman was a very skilled oarsman, with extensive local and nautical knowledge.

[4] The school was named as the *British International School* on the map of Tollesbury, 1876

neighbouring cottage opposite, of Mr and Mrs Wash, 96 East Street. Kiev noted the height and general form of the man, and believed it to have been Harrington, but he was not certain.

He thought no more of the sighting and went on his way to Salcot to his work. To Kiev and the public, now making their way to their boats and to work on the farms, it seemed like any other day in Tollesbury. It was not though, to remain that ordinary for much longer.

In 96 East Street, opposite, Mary Wash said goodbye to her brother Henry, now lodging with her and her husband John Wash. He had been with them for several months, and was finding work as a labourer on the local farms. Right now he had been engaged by a local farmer to pull up turnips. It was a relentlessly hard and difficult job, especially in the frosty November ground and some days he had not been able to earn any money as the turnips would not shift out of the ground. Lately, he had earned just 16d and it sickened him to have to earn his living that way[5]. What he really wanted to do was to emulate the trade of the oyster dredgerman. Like many men that surrounded him in East Street and elsewhere in Tollesbury, he had come to Tollesbury to be a mariner, and it was that purpose that drove Harrington on. He knew that all he needed was to buy a boat to achieve his goal, but this was going to be a difficult job in his position. Together with his close friend Abraham Emmery and another local man, Jerimiah Ketley, had agreed to buy a boat and they had found one for sale at Wivenhoe. They had already put down £1 as a deposit a month earlier and had agreed to pay off the remaining £15.10s by weekly instalments of 5 shillings between them. Today was the day they were going to Wivenhoe to see the boat for themselves. Henry was excited at the prospect of being a boat owner and one of the dredgermen, which numbered many dozens in 1850, most of them using boats owned or more likely, rented to them by the day.

---

[5] d is the sign for old pennies

Henry had risen early, before six o'clock in fact, lit his pipe and started some breakfast. John Wash had also come downstairs at that time and left almost immediately to go to his work. Henry went out to the communal privy, but found it occupied and returned to the cottage to finish getting his breakfast. The privy was used by several cottages including the Cobb's, so he did not know who was occupying it at that time, although he heard some noises coming from within to signal it was occupied. Henry said, in his typically distinguishable voice, 'OK, I'll come back later', and he returned to the cottage. Ten minutes later he tried again and met the other lodger at Wash's cottage, James Coates coming from the direction of the privy. They nodded as they passed in the passage. Henry, after using the privy, returned to the cottage and started a fire. By this time Coates together with his son, who also lodged there, had gone to their work. Henry then put on his dark plaid coat, left the cottage about a quarter to seven that morning and set off to Salcot to meet his friend Abraham Emmery, a local thatcher, who would accompany him to see Mr Horton, the boat owner at his Wivenhoe boathouse.

Mary Wash, Henry's sister, was just coming downstairs at the time that Henry had left the cottage and she heard the door close behind him. She heard the clock chime, thinking it about 6 o'clock. She would not leave the house again for several hours and did not see Henry again that day. Mary attended to her usual chores and was not disturbed until about nine o'clock, when she heard a scream coming from the Cobb's cottage opposite.

At about seven thirty, Elijah Bowles, the local fish merchant, met Henry as he was just leaving by the gate of the cottage. They exchanged nods and Elijah called out. " Have you any winkles Henry?". Henry replied, in his usually unflustered manner, "No, sorry Elijah, I don't, I've been turnipping lately, so I can't help you this week. You got a bottle of beer for me?" Elijah went inside his house and returned with a bottle and gave it to Henry.

Henry thanked him, handed over some coppers in payment, and with his head bowed, as was his usual manner, passed on by walking slowly up the street towards the Salcot footpath. Elijah noticed he was wearing a light-coloured fustian jacket over light coloured trousers, but other than that there was nothing remarkable about Henry today, and so went back to his fish-mongering.

About 8 o'clock on the footpath by the bottom of the field, just outside Salcot, Abraham Foakes, of Virley cum Salcot, saw Henry Harington arriving along the Tollesbury footpath, clearly heading for Salcot. Henry caught up with Foakes by the stile that spanned the culvert and passed on by not saying anything to him. Foakes had voiced a 'Morning Henry', but there was no acknowledgement from Henry, now deep in thought about being a boat owner. Foakes thought it was strange, as they knew each other well and Harrington was close enough to him to be heard and often chatted on his way to work. Today, Henry was silent and continuing to make his way to Salcot. Foakes went by a different route and did not see Henry again that day.

Elizabeth Orrin, a tea hawker from Stanwell Street, Colchester was in Tollesbury that morning at about eight o'clock and was knocking on the Cobb's cottage door, as she did every time she visited the village at about that time. There was no answer, which she thought strange. She tried the door, but it was locked, and she could not gain entry. As Orrin had other houses to visit she thought she would go elsewhere and come back later to see Mrs Cobb. Orrin went across the road to Mrs Wash's house, and knocked on her door. Mrs Wash answered the door. 'Any idea why Mrs Cobb isn't answering today?' Orrin enquired. Mrs Wash replied that she would try to raise her neighbour if she still needed to see Mrs Cobb. Orrin declined and went on to four other places before returning to the Cobb's place. She again tried the door, but it was still fastened. She rapped hard on the door to alert Mrs Cobb that she was present.

At the same time, Elizabeth's daughter had awoken from her dreams and got out of her cot, that was placed close to the Cobb's bed and she sat on the bed, next to her foster mother, thinking her still asleep. Elizabeth, lying on her left side was still in her night clothes and cap, but was not moving. As her daughter turned to see if she was awake she noticed that Elizabeth was covered in blood and that her throat had been cut open. She shot up and gave out a scream. At the same time, she heard a heavy rap at the door and raced downstairs shouting out in a terrified manner, "Oh, my mother is dead; my mother is dead".

Looking for someone to force the door open, Orrin started to go back to Mrs Wash's place, but noticed that the scream had alerted her also. By this time Mrs Sampson, another neighbour, hearing the commotion had also come to the Cobb's cottage to lend assistance. By this time Eliza, the distraught daughter, had passed the key through the window adjacent to the door and Mrs Wash and the other two women entered the cottage to find the child crying at the bottom of the stairs. They comforted the child before going upstairs to see what had happened. It was then that they found Elizabeth Cobb, still in bed but with all her life drained out of her. She had been brutally murdered.

The murder had apparently happened at some time between six o'clock and nine o'clock on the morning of the 25th November 1851. Elizabeth Cobb had been savagely attacked, whilst sleeping in her bed and had been struck on the head with a heavy, blunt instrument and then her throat had been severed open with a sharp instrument, such as a knife or a razor. Elizabeth had firstly been found deceased by her adopted daughter Eliza, who slept in the same room as the Cobb's and then by some of her neighbours and a visitor to her cottage in the fishing village of Tollesbury in the Essex marshes alongside the River Blackwater.

Mary Wash and another neighbour entered the house along with Mrs Orrin the tea-hawker, who had been visiting the Cobb's cottage that morning. Mary, together with Mrs Sampson, the neighbour, went upstairs, and Mary noticed some blood on the stairs as she passed upwards. She went into Mason's bedroom, which she had to do to gain access to the Cobb's bedroom. The first thing she noticed was a spot of blood on the lid of Mason's box, in which he kept his belongings. The box was open, and clothes were strewn about the floor, like someone had been eagerly searching for something. Mary crossed this room and entered the Cobb's bedroom. On the floor in front of her she noticed more blood, this time at the foot of the bed and a chill came over her entire body. She found Mrs Cobb lying in bed, half covered, in her nightclothes, cap drawn down on her head. She called out, but there was no reply. Mary lifted the sheets and instantly discovered the blood and could see that Elizabeth had had her throat cut, her nightclothes being covered in blood below her. Mary and Mrs. Sampson were in a state of shock and were joined by Mrs Orrin, closely followed by Jonathan Nicholls the local coast-guard man, who had raced from the coast-guard station a few cottages down from the Cobb's, to the cottage once he had heard what had happened. By this time quite a crowd had appeared outside the cottage.

Nicholls felt Elizabeth's face and hands, and both struck him as being cold. He noticed a trunk on the floor with some clothes scattered around it. There were no signs of what might have been used to inflict the damage to Mrs Cobb, but he thought that she most probably was killed whilst still asleep. Although he did not recall seeing any blood about the place other than on the bed, he later went back upstairs and noticed the blood that Mary had observed earlier.

During this time, someone had called for the local doctor, William Smyth, surgeon, from Tollshunt D'Arcy, a neighbouring village. Smyth arrived at the cottage at about twenty minutes past nine o'clock. He went upstairs alone and started a preliminary examination of the deceased. He noticed that Elizabeth was lying on her left side, with her left hand over her breast. Her throat had been cut and a great quantity of blood had soaked into her clothes and upon the bed under her. Examining the wound to her throat he noticed it to be about four inches in length and that the wound had severed her trachea and artery. He thought that death therefore, would have been almost instantaneous from such a vicious attack. Smyth observed also that the wound had jaggered edges and he wondered what sort of instrument might have caused this type of injury. He did see another slight wound to Elizabeth's upper lip, but did not, now, associate this with the attack on the woman. He left the cottage to write up his report, thinking he would undoubtedly be called to an inquest later that week.

Later the same day, between one and two o'clock, another local doctor, John Dawson, also of Tolleshunt D'Arcy arrived at the cottage to perform another inspection of the crime scene. He had heard of the murder via the local population, and thought he should come along to perform an initial medical investigation. He entered the woman's bedroom and started his examination, believing that the instrument that caused this terrible deed was almost surely a razor. He thought the woman must have at first been stupefied and examined her head for other inflicted wounds. Dawson noticed that Elizabeth had an indentation, a little above the right ear, which could have been made by a hammer or similar implement. This, Dawson thought, would have stupefied her prior to the neck injury having been inflicted. He also noted that the head wound had not breached the skin of the victim, but, nonetheless, surmised it could easily have rendered Elizabeth unconscious. This would also account for Elizabeth having not put up any struggle, as it now appeared was the case. Lastly, he noticed the slight wound to the upper lip.

At about three o'clock, George Watling from Salcot was standing by a stile, observing some hare coursing in the adjacent field. He saw that John Foakes, Abraham's father was on the footpath and was looking at something in a ditch, by the culvert near the stile. After about ten minutes, Foukes came over to him and said, "there looks as if there is something hid up over there, George" Returning to the ditch by the culvert, Foakes reached into the culvert and pulled out a spotted, but faded, handkerchief with something wrapped in it. He unravelled the handkerchief and found inside a cutthroat razor in a black case, both being stained in blood. He showed it to Watling and both suspected that it could be the murder weapon, given the commotion earlier that day in Tollesbury, where Elizabeth Cobb had been murdered. He wrapped it up again and said he would take it to the police. Foakes also noted the footmark on the ditch edge, but said nothing to Watling. He went off seeking the local policemen.

Meanwhile in Wivenhoe, Harrington and his friend Emmery had been to see Mr Horton, the boat owner. Finding him not at home they returned to the quay and waited about 15 minutes. Henry went again to Mr Barton's place to see the finished boat. Emmery joined him a few minutes later and both agreed that the boat's well was not deep enough for the task of oyster dredging. Barton said he would make it deeper and that they should come back when it was finished. It had been a bit of a wasted journey, and Henry felt a bit deflated, but Mr Barton took them both to the Ship at Launch public-house, where they feasted on some bread and cheese together with several pots of beer, most of which was paid for by Mr. Barton.

Mary Ann Wenlock, a servant working in the bar, served Harrington two pints of Porter that afternoon, for which he had paid with a half-crown and she had given him 1s. 10d in change. She had never seen him before, but was instantly interested when he started showing his money around.

They finished their late lunch, it was at least three o'clock, and at that time William Elijah Walford, a local cordwainer, came and sat over and sat next to Harrington. Henry had acknowledged his presence and they started up a conversation. They talked about work for a few minutes and then Harrington said, "if I can get a berth, I will go to sea. I hate the idea of working upon the land for sixteen pence a day!" Walford thought no more about it at the time, but once Harrington and Emmery had left the bar he mentioned it to Mr Barton, whom he knew very well as one of his customers.

When they at last moved, Henry and Abraham set off all the way back to Salcot, where Emmery had lodgings. Reaching the village between seven and eight o'clock in the evening, and exhausted from their travels, they stopped off at Young's public-house and ate some sprats for dinner, that Harrington had purchased in Wivenhoe. Going on to the Rising Sun at about nine o'clock.

Back in Tollesbury, it was being rumoured that Henry Harrington had been missing from the village all day. It seems he was not a trusted person to many of the villagers, some saying that he had a certain manner about him and was anyway, as was the talk in the village, that he was of bad character. No explanation was given to this feeling, but it had stuck in the heads of some villagers. There was of course no evidence at that point to suspect him other than by circumstantial evidence, but once Fox, the local constable had made some enquiries, suspicion turned to Henry Harrington as the culprit. When Foakes turned up with the razor and the bloodstained handkerchief, opinion was that Harrington should be arrested on suspicion of wilful murder.

Meanwhile Harrington was drinking in the tap-room of the Rising Sun with Emmery, Charles Last, a local miller, and some other men. They were discussing the murder at Tollesbury. Harrington said, "It appears impossible to me that anyone could have gone up and murdered the woman without waking the child. After all, she lay just two feet from the bed." He exclaimed to the group. Wood, another of Harrington's drinking companions, said, "it was just a step away".

Constable Fox had travelled to Salcot and had found Henry Harrington drinking at the Rising Sun that evening. "I've been expecting you Constable, I've been waiting here for you to arrive", shouted out Henry, as the Constable walked into the bar. "We need to have a private chat Henry", retorted Fox and took him to a quiet room to be searched, telling Henry he was under suspicion of murder. At this point Henry did not get upset or frustrated at this accusation, but co-operated fully with the Constable. Emptying his pockets, Fox counted 1s 5d in change on him. "Strip off please Henry. I need to inspect your clothing", said Fox, lighting a candle to see by. Henry took off his outer clothing and the Constable started to examine his shirt. He found that there were no traces of blood on the shirt nor on its sleeves. He also noted that the shirt sleeves were of the short variety. Fox turned his attention to the trousers that Harrington was wearing. The rear at the top was covered in mud, now dried, and asked, "how did you get them so muddy Henry?".

Harrington replied calmly, "Coming to Salcot, I slipped on the sea wall on the way from Wivenhoe and ended up on my butt. What is all this about Constable Fox, is it because that murder near my lodgings?"

"It is Henry, so how come you have mud on both sides if you slid down on your butt? Not answering, Henry asked, "are you questioning me about that murder this morning near to my lodgings?

Ignoring Harrington's question, Fox continued, "tell me what time you left Tollesbury this morning?" "About seven o'clock, probably a little before seven I think", answered Henry.

"Did you see anyone come to the house this morning before you left? questioned Fox. "No", was the reply. "Look Henry, a very serious crime has been committed and you must present yourself at the King's head in Tollesbury at eleven o'clock tomorrow morning to attend an inquest on poor Mrs Wash's demise. "OK" replied Harrington, "me and Emmery are coming to Tollesbury tomorrow at about ten o'clock, and I assure you I will be at the King's Head by eleven".

Constable Fox finally left, thinking to himself on the way out, that Harrington had been very calm during this interview and had even given the impression of an innocent man at all times. Shortly afterwards, Harrington went to bed, sleeping in Emmery's room till the Wednesday morning.

Wednesday, 26th November 1851

Harrington and Emmery rose much later than usual and attended to their breakfast. William Beckwith, Tollesbury Constable, and an associate of Constable Fox, was going to Colchester today. On his way he stopped off at the Rising Sun in Salcot. He had heard that his associate had interviewed Harrington the evening before, and decided to see Henry Harrington for himself. He found Henry eating in the bar, alongside Emmery. Harrington, Emmery and the owner Edward

Young, were talking about the murder, but as soon as he arrived the three stopped talking about it.

At nine o'clock, Beckwith entered the Rising Sun, before the two had even finished their breakfast.

"Hello Henry", said Beckwith, "you have to come to Tollesbury with me". "OK, I told Constable Fox I would be there, but I will go with you once I finish my breakfast", replied Henry, gulping down his last mouthful.

Beckwith then returned to Tollesbury with Harrington and during the journey he remained silent about the murder. He took the prisoner to his house, where Constable Fox was waiting, together with Superintendent Cook, the senior police officer. Henry was then taken into the custody of Constable Fox. He stood against the fire to light his pipe and Beckwith then noticed some spots of red, which he thought was ink, on the right leg of his fustian trousers. Each spot had a white outer ring around it, he noticed, which Beckwith took to be chalk. "What are those spots Henry?", he asked. Looking down, pipe in mouth, Henry gave no reply.

Meanwhile, the talk in Tollesbury that morning was that the weapon, the one found by Foakes in the culvert, was a razor and it looked just like the one owned by John Wash, some folks had said. Naturally, the village then gossiped that it was the murder weapon, as it had blood all over it, as did the pink spotted handkerchief accompanying it.

Charles Cook was the Superintendent of Police at Witham, where the news had been received with some shock and attention to official procedures. He immediately went to Tollesbury to oversee the investigation. On arrival, he was met by Constable Fox, who was awaiting the return of Constable Beckwith with the suspect. After some initial questioning at Beckwith's house, Harrington had been placed in the village lock-up, adjacent to St. Mary's church in the square. After being handed over to Superintendent Cook, he was taken to the Plough and Sail public-house to interview him. He also examined Harrington's trousers and noticed some spots of what he took to be blood, on the right thigh. "Where did those come from

Henry?" he said. "I don't know how they came to be there", replied Henry calmly. "I did carry a pig's pluck home recently, so maybe they came from there", he continued[6]. "I haven't done anything wrong Superintendent, I'm innocent", stated Harrington as he was being locked up again.

Cook, accompanied by another Police Officer, George Archer, then visited the Wash's cottage, where Henry lodged with his sister and her husband. He found two coats, two waistcoats and two pairs of trousers. He also found two blue pocket handkerchiefs, and a clean shirt in Henry's bedroom. He asked Mrs Wash, and she confirmed that these were all the belongings that Henry possessed in the house at that time. She saw the handkerchiefs and told the Superintendent that one of the blue handkerchiefs belonged to her husband. Cook left the house at that point, thinking it not being required to search further, as Mrs Wash had stated that what he had found was all of Henry's belongings.

When he inspected the jacket, he noticed a red smear upon the lining of the right-hand pocket, and thought it might be blood. He found two large spots of red on a pair of Harrington's trousers as well, again on the inside right-hand pocket lining. The latter had gone through the lining and soaked the jacket's flap. Cooke thought that it was enough evidence to detain Harrington and took him in to custody pending charges. He took Harrington back to the Witham police station for charging and placing on remand.

Thursday, 27th November 1851

On Thursday a post-mortem examination of the deceased was held by the two Surgeons that had attended the cottage earlier in the week. A third Surgeon, Mr Tomlinson was also in attendance. Dawson inspected the blow to the head and discovered that it was far more extensively damaged than they had first announced. This wound on the head showed signs of a shattering of the fragile temporal bone, into ten or twelve fragments. He also noted that the skin and muscles

---

[6] Pluck is an old word for offal.

surrounding the wound were of such a state that he thought the blow would have been given prior to the neck wound having been inflicted. This was not though, where he had thought the blunt instrument had penetrated. At that point, a round indentation existed, which may have been inflicted by a hammer or similar instrument. Dawson thought that this wound would not likely be the cause of death. He was even doubtful that a hammer was the weapon used, since a hammer was more likely to force the bones into the brain, which it had not.

Dawson noted that the yoke of the temporal bone, or cheek bone, was also broken and it was unlikely that one blow could have caused both wounds. It was possible, he thought, that more than one blow was inflicted on the victim whilst she slept in her bed. If that was the case, maybe a lighter weapon was used. He did not wish to speculate further. Dawson then turned his attention to the throat wound, forming the opinion that it had been inflicted with a sharp instrument such as a razor.

Next, Mr William Smyth examined the deceased. He came to the same conclusions as Mr Dawson, that several blows must have been inflicted to have caused the damage to the skull and cheek bone. He then admitted that he had revisited the cottage later on the Tuesday afternoon to re-examine the body. He examined the throat on the Tuesday and was of the opinion that it had not been inflicted with a razor. There were jaggered edges to the wound and a razor would not cause such wounds. He had since, changed his mind, having observed that these 'jags' he had noticed on the Tuesday, were on the skin and not within the flesh below. The wound was such that it might have been inflicted by a razor and the 'jags' could be explained by way of how the attacker had inflicted them. He suggested that the culprit could not have kept the razor steady.

Whatever the method, both Surgeons agreed that at the very least the culprit's shirtsleeves were likely to have been stained by the blood flow, which would have been extensive given the position of the wound. Finishing up, Smyth insisted that the head wound was most probably caused by something like a hammer, the indentation being perfectly circular. He therefore remained at odds to his fellow Surgeon.

Friday, 28th November 1851

On Friday morning the prisoner Harrington was taken before the magistrate W. W. Luard, Esq., at the Witham police station, and formally charged with the murder of Elizabeth Cobb. Cook detailed the grounds upon which the prisoner had been taken into custody, but stated that further time was required to get together additional evidence. The prisoner was, therefore, remanded till Thursday. 4th December, the following week.

Saturday, 29th November 1851

During the day Constable Fox got to work seeking out possible murder weapons. He went to the cottage where the murder had taken place and searched around for possible instruments. He went out the back of the property and searched the osier ground about 25 yards to the rear and opposite the cottage's back window. He knew the osier ground had not previously been searched. He found lying on the ground a broken hedge stake that had been removed from its hole in the hedgerow. Picking the stake up he placed the stake into the hole and it was a perfect fit. Someone he deduced, had removed the stake recently, and discarded it not far from where it had been taken. He thought the find might be significant and mulled over whether he should present it as evidence for the investigation. Fox then went back indoors and on the windowsill of the deceased's rear window sill he found a piece of bark, the size of a finger nail, not dissimilar to the bark on the hedge stake. Both, he surmised, were elm and when held together they matched. He discarded the piece of bark, but held on to the stake as it was going to be valuable evidence, even though he found no actual elm wood in the deceased's cottage.

3 The Inquest

This foregoing reconstruction is based on the Coroner's inquest reports in both local and national newspapers. The following account is the actual reports as they appeared in the newspapers and were read by the public during and following this case. The clearest reports have been chosen to best describe the inquest outcome. All the grammar and spelling are as appeared in the newspapers of the time.

An inquest was hurriedly put together for the day after the murder, to be held at the King's Head, at Tollesbury. The murder had stirred up a great deal of interest locally and from further afield. At least one newspaper man was present to record the affair. There was hardly standing room in the King's Head room, where the inquest was to be held. The Coroner appointed was William Codd Esq. and he was seated at one end of the room, with a respected Jury alongside him. Exactly how they managed to get a Jury together so quickly is not known, but I suspect it was made up of villagers from the local area. Everyone had to fight for position in the room, with both spectators and witnesses alike competing for a seat. Harrington was brought into the room after having to walk through a crowd outside, baying for his blood. It seemed the crowd had already made their minds up who was to blame.

Evidence was given in no order of events, with James Cobb being deposed first. It is remarkable that even the *Edinburgh Courant* published the report, which summarises events at Tollesbury, from the Essex newspaper reports and could print the story on the Saturday of the same week.

ATROCIOUS MURDER AT TOLLESBURY

An atrocious murder has been committed at Tollesbury, a fishing village lying upon the marshes of the Blackwater. The victim is the wife of an oyster dredgerman, James Cobb, thirty-three years of age, who was murdered while asleep in her bed, after her husband had left her, early Tuesday morning. The victim was found in bed apparently in the position in which she had been sleeping, with an indentation in her skull, several other wounds on her head, and her throat cut, life being extinct. The object of the crime was clearly plunder; and the presumption is that, having entered by the window, he proceeded up the stairs, struck his victim with a hammer on the head as she lay asleep, and having rendered her insensible, cut her throat with a razor. The murderer then appeared to have ransacked the boxes in this and another room in search of money, but he did not succeed in finding more than 12s, which was taken away, a tea caddy, containing about the same sum, still standing close to the bed of the murdered woman, having escaped his search. The dreadful death produced awful excitement throughout the village and the adjacent parishes; and suspicion soon pointed to Henry Harrington, a young man about twenty years of age, who lodged in a house adjoining. A hammer belonging to the person at whose house he lodged has been found exactly to fit the indentation in the head of the deceased; and a labourer, at Salcot, two miles off, found in the woolve of a stile, a handkerchief and a razor in a case, both bloody, the former of which had been identified as belonging to Henry Harrington, and the razor being the property of Wash, with whom he lodged, and who, on going to look for it, found it was gone[7]. It was further found that the prisoner's trousers were marked with spots of blood. He remains in custody at the police-station at Witham[8].

---

[7] Woolve or Wolf, an arch or culvert of water to pass through. From the Anglo-Saxon *hwealf, hwolf*, convexity, arch. Cognate to this are the German, *Gewölte*; English, vault. This word was repeated

[8] *Edinburgh Evening Courant*, Saturday 29 November 1851

Another report a day earlier in the *London Daily News*, also taken from the *Chelmsford Chronicle* stated:

With feelings of humiliation and sorrow, we have to add the details of another atrocious murder to the bloodstained deeds which have blackened the criminal annals of the county within the last few years. The scene of the horrid tragedy in this case is Tollesbury, a considerable fishing village, lying upon the marshes of the Blackwater, and close to Tiptree-heath, and the victim is the wife of an oyster dredgerman, named James Cobb, thirty-three years of age, who was murdered while asleep in her bed, after her husband had left her, early on Tuesday morning. Cobb was employed in the oyster laying, of which there is a considerable extent in the neighbourhood, and it appears left her for his work about six o'clock in the morning, a lodger having previously quitted the house, the wife being at the time awake, a little girl, seven years old, whom they had adopted, having no children of their own, slept in a crib close to the bed. Other homes adjoin, but nothing was heard to create alarm or excite surprise, till eight o'clock, when the little girl awoke, and finding the woman dead gave the alarm and admitted the neighbours. The victim was then found lying in the bed, apparently in the position in which she had been sleeping, with an indentation in her skull, several other wounds to her head, and her throat cut, life being extinct. The object of her murderer was clearly plunder, and the presumption is, that having entered by the window, he proceeded upstairs, struck his victim with the hammer in the head as she lay asleep, and rendered her insensible, cut her throat with a razor, thus affecting the murder without awaking the child, that lay slumbering within a few feet, and who, if she had been disturbed, would probably have been silenced in the same summary manner. The murderer then appears to have ransacked the boxes in that and another room in search of money, but he did not succeed in finding more than 12s, belonging to the lodger, which was taken away, a tea caddy, containing about the same sum, standing close to the bed of the murdered woman having escaped his search.

The dreadful deed produced awful excitement throughout the village and the adjacent parishes: the police were early on the spot, investigating all the circumstances, and suspicion soon pointed to Henry Harrington, a young man about twenty years of age, who lodged in a house adjoining, as it was ascertained he had not quitted his house till after Cobb and his landlord had gone, and this same morning proceeded to Wivenhoe. The evidence against him at first appeared extremely slight, but the officer felt it his duty to take him into custody, and facts have since come out that lend strongly to fix him with the guilt. A hammer belonging to the person at whose home he lodged has been found exactly to fit the indentation in the head of the deceased: & on Wednesday, a labourer at Salcot, 2 miles off, found in the woulves of a stile, in the direction the prisoner went to Wivenhoe, a handkerchief and a razor in a case, both bloody, the former of which has been identified as belonging to Harrington, and the razor is the property of Wash, with whom he lodged, and who, on going to look for it, found it was gone. It was further found that the prisoner's trowsers were marked with spots of blood, and it appeared that he had attempted to hide some by putting ink over them. He remains in custody at the poice-station, at Witham; though youthful in look, he has a determined and somewhat foreboding appearance. He has been sometimes employed as a labourer on a farm, and at other times as an assistant in dredging. The husband of the murdered woman, though in humble life, occupied a respectable position in the village. Superintendents May and Cook, with several active officers under them, are taking charge of the further inquiries into the case, and yesterday, Capt. Me Hardy, the Chief of Police himself was throughout the day at Tollesbury prompting the investigation[9].

The *Chelmsford Chronicle* report on Friday 28th November 1851 added the following information concerning the inquest, which had been hurriedly convened for Wednesday 26th at Tollesbury[10]:

---

[9] *London Daily News*, Friday 28th November 1851

[10] *Chelmsford Chronicle*, Friday 28th November 1851

THE INQUEST

On Wednesday, an inquest was held at the King's Head Inn, Tollesbury, before Wm. Codd, Esq., coroner, and a respectable jury, when, after viewing the body, the following evidence was admitted ---

James Cobb of Tollesbury, dredgerman deposed: The deceased, Elizabet Cobb, was my wife and was thirty-three years of age; I had been married to her for about eight years, but had no child by her; a little girl whom I adopted a few years since, named Elisa Spurgin, lived with us; two men, named Edward Peates and William Mason, both dredgermen, lodged in the house, the little girl, Elisa Spurgin, slept in the same room with my wife and myself, in a crib near the bed; about a quarter before six o'clock the following morning (yesterday the 25th inst.) I got up and went down stairs; William Mason who lodged in the room through which I passed, had already gone down stairs, my wife was awake when I went down stairs, but the child was asleep, before I went down stairs, my wife asked me at what time I should be home: I put my arm round her, and kissing her, said, 'At half-past one'; nothing further passed: I left the house as soon as I had booted, which was about six o'clock. I left the house by the door, and I went down to the river to my work: Mason left the house about five minutes before me, and went to the same spot where I found him. Between one and two o'clock the same afternoon I was coming from my work, I was informed my wife had been murdered, no suspicion came across my mind as to who could have murdered her; on my arrival at home, I went upstairs and found my wife lying in bed in her night clothes with her throat cut, and quite dead: I found that my box in the bedroom had been nearly emptied of its contents, containing chiefly clothing, which laid upon the floor; a tea-caddy stood upon the drawers, by the bedside, which contained 12s.; it was locked and had not been touched. In the adjoining room (Mason's) I found his box also open, and some of his clothing lying upon the floor; there was a till inside the box, which had been broken open. Pewter, when at home, slept in his room, his box I found also open; from the appearance of the window sill of the room down stairs, I thought that somebody had been through it, as I saw a leaf and a small piece of bark on the window sill which were shown to me by the policeman: the window was quite large enough for a good-sized man to get through; I have often got through the window myself to clean the flower garden; I get through the window at such times as the passage to it round the corner of the house was blocked and I have put my wife through for the same purpose. I placed the razor behind a tray on the table down stairs, where I had kept it for the last month. I found the razor in the same place where I had put it, it did not appear to have been used since I last used it myself; Mason's razor was also found in his room, and appeared quite clean. I had no reason then, nor have I any reason now, to suspect any one of having committed the deed. I have heard that a man named Henry Harrington, who lodged next door to me, is in custody on suspicion, but I never saw him in my house that I recollect; my wife was not in the habit of locking the house door that I know of after I left home.

Mary Wash, the wife of John Wash of Tollesbury, dredgerman, deposed, I live in the house opposite to that of the deceased; yesterday morning, the 25th inst. about 8 o'clock, I heard the little girl, Elisa Spurgin, scream out, and I went to the door, which I found locked; she told me her mother (meaning deceased) was dead, and I and Mrs. Sampson, a neighbour, went in together and went upstairs, where we found the deceased lying in bed in her night clothes, upon her left side; I could only see part of her face, as it was nearly covered up by the sheets; I took off the sheet and then saw that her throat was cut and her clothes covered with blood: I did not feel her, and cannot say whether her body was cold or warm; about seven o'clock I heard someone pass my door, who might have come from the back part of Cobb's house; Henry Harrington, my brother who lodges with me, left my house that morning about a quarter of an hour or twenty minutes before seven; It might be either more or less; he was going to Salcot, and then to Wivenhoe: I knew some days before that he was going to Wivenhoe to fetch a boat, which he and others were going to buy amongst them, which was understood to have been paid for by instalments of a shilling a week each. My brother got up that morning about six o'clock, and I believe left the house about a quarter before seven: I heard the footsteps of someone passing my house about a quarter of an hour afterwards. When I first went up into the room, I was not alarmed that I did not observe anything particular in it; but on going up a few minutes afterwards, I saw a large box in Cobb's room open, and a quantity of clothing lying upon the floor: I also saw two boxes in the adjoining room, also open, and a quantity of clothing scattered about the floor: I have no suspicion whatever as to who can have committed the deed; the hammer now produced belonged to me: I kept it in the coal house; the last time I saw it there was on Saturday or Sunday last, I cannot say which; no one can get to the coal house without coming into my room, and no one came into the house after my brother left, but Mrs. Orrin: no one could have come into the house after my brother left without being seen by me, as I did not leave my room. The deceased and her husband always lived very comfortably together, ---- no couple could have lived more so: I have known them for upwards of two years; I could see no instrument in the room with which the wound on the throat of the deceased could have been inflicted.

Johnathan Nicholls, of Tollesbury, coast-guard man, examined. Yesterday morning, the 25th inst. A little before nine o'clock, I heard that the deceased was lying with her throat cut; I went to the house, and upstairs I found two or three women in the room; upon the bed I saw the deceased, lying with her throat cut; I felt her face and hands, and both were cold, but I did not feel her body; I saw a trunk lying in the bedroom open, and some clothes scattered upon the floor; in the adjoining room were also two boxes open, and clothes lying upon the floor; I did not see any instrument in the room with which the wound on the throat of the deceased could have been inflicted; from the position in which I found the deceased lying, it appeared to me that her throat had been cut whilst she was asleep: I did not observe any blood upon the floor at the time, but on going up about half an hour afterwards, I saw a spot of blood upon the floor, near the chest of drawers and about three-quarters of a yard from the bed; I also saw a spot of blood upon the stairs, about half way down.

Mary Wash, on being re-examined, stated --- When I first went into the room, I saw a spot of blood upon the floor, near the foot of the bed and close to the box; I also saw a drop of blood upon the outside of the lid of Mason's box, in the next room, and also another spot of blood upon the stairs.

William Smyth, of Tollshunt D'Arcy, surgeon, examined. Yesterday morning, about nine o'clock, I was called upon to go and look at the deceased; I arrived at the house about twenty minutes or half-past nine; on going upstairs I found the deceased lying in bed in her night clothes; she was lying upon her left side; the left hand was lying upon her breast; her throat was cut and a great quantity of blood was upon her clothes and upon the bed under her; I examined the wound, it was an incised wound about four inches in length; the trachea and oesophagus were both divided, and I should say death must have been almost instantaneous: I am of opinion from the appearance of the edges of the wound, that it could not have been inflicted with a razor, as they are a little jaggered. I cannot say whether the cut was made from right to left or from left to right; there was also a small wound upon her upper lip. I did not then examine the head, but I have this day done so, and above the right ear and a little in front I found a fracture of the skull, about the circumference of a half-penny, which appeared to have been inflicted by a violent blow from some blunt instrument, probably a hammer; such a blow might have been inflicted by the hammer now produced; and must have been followed by immediate insensibility; I also found two contused wounds upon the scalp, one of which was a slight fracture of the upper jaw; it is quite impossible that these wounds could have been given by herself; I diligently searched the apartment for some instrument or instruments which might have occasioned the wounds described, but found nothing; my immediate impression upon seeing her was, that she must have been killed during her sleep.

Wm Mason, of Tollesbury, dredgerman. I have been lodging in Cobb's house for about two years and a half, and slept there on the night of Monday last, and in a room adjoining, in which Cobb and his wife slept; I got up the next morning (Tuesday, the 25th,) between six and seven o'clock and went down stairs, and as soon as I had put on my boots I went to the privy, and while there I heard someone coming down the path towards the privy; thinking he might be coming in, I made a noise which was answered by the person whom I took by his voice to be Henry Harrington; the privy was common to three or four cottages near, of which Harrington's cottage was one; as soon as I left , I went indoors again to get my jacket and almost immediately after left to my work; I think it was about half-past six; Cobb was then down stairs. I don't think when I went to the privy that I was absent from the house more than five minutes; no one slept in the house on Monday night but Cobb and his wife, the little girl Spurgin and myself; in the room where I slept I had a box containing my clothes; it was not locked, and at the top of the box on the inside a till was affixed, which I left locked, and put the key under the till; the till contained about twelve shillings in silver, consisting of two or three halfpence, and when I returned home yesterday I found the till broken open and all the money gone; my clothes, which were found upon the floor, I placed upon the top of the box yesterday morning; I called Cobb yesterday morning (the 25th inst.) as soon as I got out of bed, and almost immediately afterwards he gave me a light; I did not observe whether or not he was dressed; I heard nothing pass between his wife and himself that morning; Cobb and his wife have always appeared to me to live very comfortably together; I never heard them quarrel. I have no reason to believe that Cobb was jealous of his wife; some time since I sold a pair of boots to Henry Harrington for 18 pence, and about three weeks since I had some words about him, as he had only paid me sixpence; he said he would pay me as soon as he could; he still owes me a shilling for them; I never saw him in Cobb's home but once, and then he only came into the room

THE TOLLESBURY MURDER

Henry Harrington, of Tollesbury, aforesaid labourer, then in custody on suspicion, having been first duly cautioned and sworn, stated --- I live with my sister Mrs. Wash, and opposite to Cobb's house; on Tuesday morning last, the 25th inst., about six o'clock, I got up and lit my pipe, and went up the yard towards the privy, when I heard someone in there; I went indoors and began my breakfast and in about ten minutes afterwards, I again went to the privy, and met a man named James Coates, who lodges with me coming from it; I shortly after returned into the house and made a fire and finished my breakfast; Coates had then gone to his work; I left home before 7 o'clock to go to Salcot to see Abraham Emmery, who was going along with me to Wivenhoe to get a boat, and he and I went to Wivenhoe the same day; Jerimiah Ketley, Abraham Emmery and I had paid a pound down amongst us for the boat, about a month ago, and were to pay the remainder, £15 10s, by weekly instalments of five shillings amongst us; we went to the owner of the boat, Mr. Horton of Wivenhoe, and he told us the boat was ready, but when we went to look at her we found the well had not been made high enough, and we came away the same day without the boat, and reached Salcot about seven that evening, when I slept that night at the Rising Sun with Emmery; I did not come on to Tollesbury as I heard policemen Fox was after me; and I was told that he was coming to Salcot for me; I was apprehended by policemen Fox at Tollesbury, this morning, when I left house yesterday morning I had a few shilling pieces; I had two shillings of it from Rillingson, Mr. Fulhead's looker[11], and the other shilling from Mr. Wyatt a bricklayer of Tollesbury; the coat which I may have on is the same coat I wear the whole of yesterday, the 25th instant, from the time I got up; I have only two coats, and both of them are at home; I have no razor of my own, but always use John Wash's razor where I lodge; I believe it was a black handled one, but am not quite certain; I think I should know it if I was to see it again: I have not shaved with it for the last fortnight; I think I got to Salcot about 8 o'clock; I went by the road as far as Old Hall Chase and thus went along the path by the fields; I

---

[11] Looker is a name for a farm chargehand or overseer

did not leave the path at all; I have one handkerchief only; and that is at home; I should know it again if I was to see it; I have had no other since I have been of Tollesbury: I very seldom use it; I did not use it yesterday morning; I kept the handkerchief at the head of my bed; James Coates and his son slept in the same room with me, and did so on Monday night last; Coates and his son, aged about twelve years, left house before me about half an hour.

John Dawson, of Tolleshunt D'Arcy, surgeon. Yesterday afternoon between one and two o'clock, I heard that a woman had had her throat cut at Tollesbury, and I went to look at her. Going up stairs I found her lying in bed in her night clothes with her throat cut, from the position in which I found her, I felt satisfied that she must have been stupefied before her throat was cut. I do not consider the wound in the throat alone to be such as would have rendered her incapable of resistance. My impression from the appearance of the edge of the wound was that it must have been inflicted with a razor or some other sharp instrument the edge of which was somewhat convex; and I this afternoon made a sketch of it. On the head I found an indentation a little above the right ear, such a one as might have been made by a hammer now produced, and I should imagine that such a blow would have rendered her insensible. I found two lacerated wounds at the back of the right ear which might have been caused by the blow of the hammer produced. I fitted the head of the hammer to the indentation which appeared to correspond; there was no breach of the skin over the indentation; there was a clean cut wound in the upper lip; the razor now produced corresponds with the form of the edge I have sketched, and is of such a form as would have caused the wound in the throat; the skin of the wound was a little jaggered, which I attribute to the party using it being unable to keep a firm hold of the instrument; between the jags the cutting was perfectly smooth; I had not seen the razor produced previously to making the form of the supposed edges, it had not then in my knowledge been found.

THE TOLLESBURY MURDER

John Foakes, of Salcot. Labourer deposed --- This afternoon about three o'clock, I was on my way to Salcot; I went by the fields along the path; when I got to a stile within one field of Salcot, I saw a man's footmark in the ditch, and from what I had heard at Tollesbury, I thought about looking in the ditch, when I saw a handkerchief; three men whom I knew were standing by the stile watching a coursing party, and I said to them "Come and look here", and one of them, George Watling, came and I stooped down and took from a woolve a pocket handkerchief in which I found a black-handled razor in a black case, the same now produced, there was blood upon the handkerchief and also upon the razor; the razor and handkerchief are both now exactly in the same state in which I found them.

George Watling, of Salcot, labourer, examined. This afternoon, about three o'clock, I was standing by a stile within a field at Salcot with two other men watching a coursing party; the stile was by the footpath; while we were standing there, John Foakes came up to the stile, and when he had been there about ten minutes, he said "There looks as if there was something hid up", and he got down and pulled out a woolve the handkerchief now produced in which on opening, were found the razor and black case now produced; both razor and handkerchief were stained with blood; I did no see the footmarks.

John Wash, of Tollesbury, dredgerman, Henry Harrington, now in custody, lodges at my house; I have a black handled razor, which I usually keep in a black case; The last time I shaved with it was Sunday morning last, which I put that morning either on the sill of the window in the room downstairs or in the drawer, I don't recollect which; I only shave once a week; this day, about three o'clock, a policeman came and asked me for my razor, and I went to look for it, but was unable to find it. Harrington used the same room with me; I think I should know it again if I saw it; the razor now produced is like mine both in form and colour, but I cannot undertake to swear it is mine; I bought the razor at Portland, in America, about eleven years ago, and have used it ever since; when I first had the razor the was engraved upon the blade these words --- "which buys me will not repent", but I have not noticed the words for the last 8 years; it has been very often ground; the razor now produced is like the one I used, and I believe it is mine; I never saw the handkerchief now produced before to my knowledge.

The before named James Cob further stated --- I have been in the habit for upwards of twelve months past, of borrowing Master Wash's razor, and have often set it for him; it was kept in a black handled case; the case now produced is exactly like the one in which Wash kept his razor; I believe the razor now produced to be the one I have been in the habit of having from Wash; it appears to be exactly like it; I don't know anything about the handkerchief.

The before named Mary Wash, further stated --- Henry Harrington, who lodged with me, had two pocket handkerchiefs belonging to him, one of them was a blue one and the other one a white one dotted with pink; I have sometimes washed them for him, and I think I should know them again if I was to see them; the pink one was an old one; and rather faded; I cannot recollect if it had any holes in it; it was not marked with his name or initials; his handkerchief was spotted like the one now produced, and was very much like it, although I could not undertake to swear that it is his; Harrington had no particular place for keeping his handkerchiefs; he had no box, he sold it before he came to lodge with us about Christmas last.

The inquest was adjourned till Tuesday[12].

---

[12] *Chelmsford Chronicle,* Friday 28th November 1851

This report was followed with the following concerning the examination of the body:

Latest Particulars

Thursday 27th November 1851 (Evening)

Today a post-mortem examination of the body of the deceased was made by Mr. Dawson and Mr. Smith, when it was found that the injuries from the blow on the head were much more extensive than had been at first supposed, and were sufficient of themselves to cause death, inasmuch as the whole of this part of the bone on which the hammer fell was shattered to fragments.

It is a little singular that when the crime was discovered, the general feeling of the inhabitants of the village was one of suspicion against the prisoner, this being in part produced by the general character which he bore. The prisoner, it is stated, had on former occasions been heard to give utterance to threats against the deceased. It is also added that Cobb was to have been a partner in the boat alluded to in the evidence, and had stated he had his £5 ready to pay his share; it is therefore concluded the motive that instigated to the murder was to obtain possession of this money, in which however, the perpetrator did not succeed[13].

The inquest reconvened on Tuesday 2nd December 1851.

THE TOLLESBURY MURDER

Yesterday, the coroner's inquest on the body of the murdered woman, Mrs. Cobb, was resumed at the King's Head, Tollesbury, having it will be remembered, stood adjourned till that day. The excitement in the village had in no degree diminished in the interval. There was a tremendous rush for places in the room where the

---

[13] *Chelmsford Chronicle*, Friday, 28th November 1851

inquiry was conducted, and all the available space in the inn was occupied throughout the day. In fact, all ordinary business in the village appeared to be suspended. The prisoner Harrington was placed at one end of the table, under the guard of two policemen. His demeanour during the earlier part of the day was remarkably calm he did not look concerned. Though twenty years of age, he is quite a lad in appearance. He is of thick sturdy build, rather short in stature, of dark complexion, and of a resolute or dogged cast of countenance. He wore a black frock coat, not in very good condition. He was ably defended by Mr. Church, a solicitor at Maldon.

The first witness called was the prisoner's sister, with whom he lodged.

------ Wash, examined by the coroner – On the morning of the murder, the 25th ult., my husband got up a little before 6 o'clock, and left almost immediately to go to his work. Coates and his son, our lodgers, went away, I believe, at the same time. I got up about 6 o'clock. The clock was striking whilst I was dressing, and I came downstairs about half-past six. I did not go upstairs again till between 10 and 11; nor did I leave the house. My brother left the house just as I was coming downstairs. I heard him shut the door. I did not see him afterwards that day, but I saw him before he went downstairs. He had on a dark plaid coat (this was produced), and dark trowsers (also produced). He had worn these trowsers some days before the murder. I did not observe spots of any sort on his trowsers. There were three other pairs of trowsers belonging to him. One was a pair of dark tweed; another was a pair of dark fustian, which had got rather light by washing; the other I believe to have been fustian. He wore them occasionally. I never observed any spots of any kind upon any of them. I am quite sure my brother, the prisoner, never came into the house that morning after he left. I did not leave the downstairs room before 8 o'clock, and he could not have come into the house without my seeing him. The window of that room was fastened that morning; it had not been opened lately to my knowledge. I did not observe my husband's razor on the window-sill when I came downstairs. The last time I recollect seeing it was on the Sunday before the murder, and my husband was then shaving with it. I don't at all know what money he had about him when he left. Mrs. Orrin came to my house on the morning of the murder about 8 o'clock. That was before I heard the child scream.

Cross-examination by Mr. Church --- My brother, the prisoner. Helped to kill a pig about a month ago or five weeks before the murder, and he brought home part of the pig in a cloth, which had been killed a few days before. The cloth was bloody. I washed it. The three pairs of trowsers which he had besides those he wore were found in the house after the murder. I did not observe how he was dressed on the morning he brought part of the pig home. On Saturday last I found in my drawer down stairs a white handkerchief dotted with pink. It belonged to my brother, the prisoner. Yesterday (Monday) I placed it on the table before the superintendent of police. Some other person was present, but I don't know who it was. As soon as they left the house I missed the handkerchief, and I hav not seen it since.

Two handkerchiefs were then produced, one of which was stated to have been found in a field near Salcot, while the other was that supposed to having been found in her drawer last Saturday. They had a general resemblance, except the one was dirty and marked apparently with blood, and the other clean, as though recently washed. The pattern of the two was exactly the same: a white ground, with pink dots, and a pink border about an inch wide; but the one alleged to have been found in the drawer was much more faded than the other; unlike the other, it had nearly lost the original outline of the pattern.

In reply to repeated questions from the coroner, the witness said positively that the handkerchief marked with blood was not her brother's; but on being pressed to state how she knew this, she admitted that she could not have sworn that it was not his had she not found another like it in the drawer. He had only one handkerchief of that pattern.

George Archer, a policeman, examined by the coroner --- Yesterday, about 1 o'clock, I went with Superintendent Cook, to the house of John Wash, where the prisoner lodged. Mr. Cook asked Mrs. Wash how many handkerchiefs her brother, the prisoner, had? She said two, one a blue one; that Mr. Cook had taken two blue ones away, one of which belonged to her husband. She added that she had found the old pink one belonging to Henry Harrington in his drawer. She then opened a drawer and showed us the handkerchief now produced, which is similar in size and pattern to the one with blood on it. It was clean, and looked as though it had been recently washed and ironed. It was more faded than the one with blood on it. Before going to the house I had not heard anything about the finding of a handkerchief. Mrs. Wash said nothing more about the handkerchief I have mentioned. I took charge of it.

The Coroner (to Mrs. Wash) ---Do you know where your brother bought the handkerchief?

Mrs. Wash –No: he had it when he came to lodge with me, which was about last Christmas.

George Archer cross-examined by Mr. Church --- Mrs. Wash produced the handkerchief immediately after being questioned. Since yesterday morning I have not mentioned it to anyone. When given to me it was dry. I cannot say from its appearance how long it had been folded up.

By a Juryman. --- There were other clean things in the drawer.

The Coroner (to Mrs. Wash) – Why, did you not say, when the handkerchief was produced, that the dots on your brother's handkerchief were scarcely perceptible?

The witness --- Well, the soda has washed out the dots of his handkerchief.

The two handkerchiefs were here measured; their size is exactly the same.

Mr. Dawson (the surgeon examined on the previous day),

Recalled and examined by the coroner. --- On Thursday I examined the head of the deceased, by dissection, being assisted by Mr. Smith and Mr. Tomlinson. The skin and the muscles over the fracture were in such a condition that I think the blow must have been given previous to death. The upper portion of the temporal bone, which is a very thin and brittle bone, was broken into ten or twelve fragments; not having connected them I cannot state the exact number. I refer now to that part of the skull to which the hammer fitted. The blow on the temple was not sufficient to cause immediate death. I have some doubts --- more than I had --- as to the hammer being the instrument which was used. I think a blow from a heavy hammer would have forced the bones into the brain. It is possible that the hammer may have done it.

The witness here produced a human skull, which he used to explain the nature and probable effect of a blow from the hammer. The hammer is an instrument about a foot long, folk-shaped at the head, and entirely of iron.

A mallet and a hedge stake, afterwards alleged to have been found by the police, were here placed on the table. The former was a clumsy-looking tool, but not otherwise worthy of mention: while the latter, the hedge stake, was about a yard long, an inch thick, nearly covered with bark, and completely broken about the centre, as if from violent concussion.

Examination continued --- The wounds at the back did not penetrate below the skin. I doubt whether the hedge stake before me would have produced the marks on the head. Had that been used, I think the wound would have been longer.

Mr. Church said if these article were to be used against the optioned, they must be made the subject of regular evidence.

Mr. Dawson's examination continued --- If the hammer was used there must have been repeated blows with it. The extremity of the yoke of the temporal bone was broken. It is possible that the hedge stake produced may have made such a wound, but with so light an instrument the blow must have been given with great force. I have no reason to alter my previously expressed opinion, that the wound in the throat was inflicted with a razor. Several more scratches have become apparent as the body has decomposed. I believe a sharp instrument was used with a slightly convex edge. I think it possible for a party inflicting such a wound with a razor to have made it without having his shirt or shirt-sleeves stained with blood; this, however, is not possible. There was no rupture of the membranes of the brain.

Cross-examined by Mr. Church --- It is my opinion that the blows on the head rendered the deceased insensible; if no other wound had been given she might possibly have lived some hours, or even days. It is a delicate thing to say what instrument produced death. If the hammer was used there must have been several blows. My impression is rather that the hammer was not used; I am disposed to think that the instrument used was not so heavy. It is possible that the matter produced was the instrument used; this remark to the hedge stake. Had the case been one of suicide I should have supposed a razor to have been used. If there was a struggle the murderer must have run a risk of cutting himself.

Mr. William Smithe examined --- I assisted Mr. Dawson in examining the skull, and I agree with him with regard to it. On the afternoon of the day of my first examination I again examined the wound in the throat of the deceased. I see no reason to alter the opinion I first gave that it was not inflicted with an instrument so sharp as a razor. The jags which I first observed, about the wound were on the skin, and not in the flesh. I consider it possible that the wound was inflicted with a razor. The jags may have been occasioned by the party holding the razor not being able to keep it steady. The inner surface of the wound was a little uneven, but the wound might still have been inflicted with a razor. The unevenness might have been occasioned by the unsteadiness with which the instrument was held. I agree with Mr. Dawson with regard to the flow of blood from the wound, and the probability of the hands and clothes of the party inflicting the wounds being stained.

Cross-examined --- I believe that the cutting of the throat would alone occasion death. Of the three instruments, the hammer, or some such instrument, is most likely to have occasioned the blow on the head. I have still considerable doubt whether the wound in the throat was inflicted with a razor; the impression on my mind is that it was not. My opinion is unavoidably influenced by discoveries made since the last examination. The body was not cold when I first saw it. The deceased might then have been dead two hours or more. This would depend on temperature and a variety of causes. In my opinion, it is very improbable that the blows were given with the hedge stake which has been produced. The impression on the scalp was perfectly circular. And I do not think it probable that it was caused by the hedge stake.

Charles Fox, examined by the Coroner. --- On Saturday last I found the hedge stake which has been produced in an osier ground at the back of deceased's house; it was broken as it is now. In the hedge at the back of the house I found a hole from which a hedge stake appeared to have been recently drawn. I put the hedge stake to the hole, and it fitted the hole exactly. That was the first time the osier ground was searched. The stake produced is elm. On the window sill of deceased house I found a piece of bark, about the size of a finger nail; it was precisely similar to the bark on the stake. I thought it at the time, and did not keep it. I found no piece of elm wood in the house of the deceased. I am the party who apprehended the prisoner.

Cross-examined by Mr. Church --- The osier ground is about five and twenty yards from the deceased cottage. I found the stake exactly opposite the back window.

Elizabeth Orrin, examined by the Coroner. --- I am a widow and live in Stanwell Street, Colchester. On the morning of the 25th inst. I was at Tollesbury. At five minutes past eight on that morning I went to the house of James Cobb, to sell some tea, being a hawker. I tried the door, and found it fastened. I directly went to Mrs. Wash's house, and inquired whether Mrs. Cobb was out, as I had never found the door fastened, though I had frequently called there as early as 7 or 8 o'clock. Mrs. Wash then said that if I wanted her she would call her, but I said I had got two or three places to go to, and I would call again. Then I went to four places, and stopped about ten minutes at each. In about forty minutes I returned to Mrs. Cobb's. I tried the door, as before, and found it fastened. I then rapped a loud rap, and directly after I heard a child scream out, saying, "Oh, my mother is dead; my mother is dead." I then went to see if I could find someone to force open the door. I could not find any one; and on returning, almost immediately, I found that Mrs. Wash had got a key. Mrs. Wash, Mrs. Sampson, and myself went in together. That is all I know of the matter.

The court adjourned for a quarter of an hour.

On the inquiry being resumed

Elijah Bowles, was examined by the coroner. --- He said: I live in Tollesbury, and am a fish merchant. At about half-past seven on the morning of the murder, I met Henry Harrington coming out of the gate of the house where he lodged. He had on, I think, a fustian coat. I am sure it was not a dark one. His trowsers were a light colour. He was not walking very fast. He was going up the street towards Salcot.

The prisoner – I called at your house and got a pint of beer.

Examination continued --- As he passed me I asked him if he had any winkles to sell. He said, "He hadn't --- he was a turnipping," meaning, I suppose, that he was employed in pulling turnips. I have nothing more to say.

Cross-examined by Mr. Church --- When I spoke to the prisoner he did not seem at all agitated or flurried. He carried his head down, as he usually does. The plaid coat produced in court this morning is not like that which the prisoner wore. I will not swear that it is not the one he wore. I think the one he wore was lighter, but I can't state positively. There was no weapon of any kind in his hand.

The prisoner here made some remark to Mr. Church.

In reply to a question from Mr. Church, the witness said he did not know whether the prisoner had any beer at his house.

Abraham Foakes, examined by the coroner. --- I live at Salcot, and am a labourer. On the morning of the murder, about 8 o'clock, I was at the bottom of a field adjoining the street of Salcot. At 30 or 40 rods I saw Henry Harrington coming along the field on the footpath. I was going before him, and he passed me in the path. I said, "Morning Henry," but he passed on and said nothing. As I had known him for some time, I thought it strange that he did not speak, but supposed that he might not hear me. He then went along the path to Salcot. As soon as he passed, I left the field to go home a different way. When I first saw him, he was past the stile where the razor and handkerchief were found. We had generally stopped and spoken to each other, when we met. I said, "Good morning," quite loud enough for him to hear. When I spoke to him he was about half a rod from me. I am sure he saw me. I cannot say whether he knew me. I was dressed as I usually am.

The witness was then cross-examined, but did not vary from his previous statements.

The above evidence carried the inquiry up to 5 o'clock, at which hour there were about a dozen witnesses to be examined. The coroner had previously intimated that even if the witnesses in attendance could be all examined that day, there must be another adjournment to afford time for collecting additional evidence.

As the examination proceeded in the after part of the day, the prisoner's manner became less calm, and he evinced his anxiety by frequently making suggestions to Mr. Church, and interposing little comments on the evidence. The inquiry was still proceeding when the last train left for London[14].

A report in both the *Chelmsford Chronicle* and the *Essex Standard* on the 5th December 1851 covered the rest of the inquest from that day up to the adjournment and there onwards at the reconvened inquest. The *Chelmsford Chronicle* report is of poor quality, so the next phase will be reported from the *Essex Standard*.

Before providing a detailed report of the reconvened inquiry, the *Essex Standard* conveyed some more facts that had emerged since the last adjournment.

The police have since been energetically engaged in prosecuting the necessary inquiry, and have in the interval succeeded in accumulating a chain of circumstantial facts, upon which, as will be seen below, the Coroner's Jury have come to the conclusion that the man Harrington is the guilty party.

On Friday morning the prisoner Harrington was taken before W. W. Luard, Esq., at the Witham police station, formally charged with the murder. Mr. Supt. Cook detailed the grounds upon which the prisoner had been taken into custody, but stated that further time was required to get together additional evidence. The prisoner was, therefore, remanded till yesterday (Thursday).

In the meantime a post-mortem examination of the head has been made by Messrs. Dawson, Smyth, and Tomlinson, the result of which will be found detailed in the subjoined report.

Inquiries were made by the police at Wivenhoe, where they ascertained that the prisoner changed half-crowns at two public-houses, thus at once contradicting his own statement, when before the Coroner, to the effect that he started out with three shillings. A

---

[14] *London Daily News*, Wednesday, 3rd December 1851.

THE TOLLESBURY MURDER

witness, it was ascertained, had heard the prisoner make use of a threat towards the deceased woman; another was able to prove that the prisoner, on his way to Salcot, kept to the footpath, by which he must necessarily have passed the ditch in which the razor and handkerchief were found; and other evidence was collected which materially strengthened the case against the prisoner. These inquiries have been persuaded by Capt. Cooke, the Supt. of the Division, assisted by Mr. Supt. May, of Chelmsford, and police-constables Fox and Archer, acting under direction of Capt. McHardy, the chief constable, who, we understand, also devoted a day at Tollesbury to the personal investigation of the affair.

On the first discovery of the murder a measure of suspicion appears to have rested upon unfortunate husband of the deceased, and not perhaps unnaturally so, from the early hour of the day at which the disclosure was made, and from the fact that he was the last person known to have left the house. Circumstances, however, soon negitived this impression, and the prisoner Harrington (being, it is said, considered a young man of bad character) was at once inquired for; his absence from the village of course to some extent confirmed the suspicion that he was implicated in the affair, although, as we have before stated, the circumstances against him were not by any means of a cogent nature, until the accidental discovery of the razor and handkerchief.

On Tuesday morning the Coroner, W Codd, Esq., and Jury (of whom Mr. Robert Seabrook acted as foreman), reassembled at the King's Head Inn, Tollesbury, to continue their investigation into the circumstances of the murder.

The inquest room was literally besieged throughout the day, and showed the intense excitement which the occurrence had occasioned in the neighbourhood.

The arrival of the prisoner was watched with mush interest. He is as we have already stated about 20 years of age, and his personal appearance and the formation of his features are somewhat extraordinary. He is about five feet high and of thick-set and muscular frame, and an expression of countenance by no means prepossessing or agreeable. He was dressed rather after the style of a respectable farm-labourer, in black surtout coat, check waistcoat, and fustian trousers. He stood with his head inclined downwards and generally manifested an air of indifference, except occasionally when in communication with his professional adviser (Mr Church, of Colchester), to whom he addressed his instructions in the course of evidence apparently in a tone of confidence.

The Jury having answered to their names,

The Coroner said, before they proceed to hear any further evidence he proposed briefly to revert to that taken on the former occasion, or at least that which immediately preceded the evidence of Mr. Dawson, inasmuch as at that point the party suspected, as well as the Jury and himself, had been somewhat taken by surprise in the discovery of the handkerchief and the razor. He would therefore, read over the depositions of Mr. Dawson and the subsequent witness, in order that the Jury or the prisoner, having now had ample time for reflection, might ask such questions of the witnesses as they might think fit.

The deposition of John Foakes was accordingly first read over, and he was then cross-examined by Mr. Church. It was about 3 o'clock I was at the ditch in which I found the razor; I had nothing to do with and was watching the coursing party; I was attracted by a foot-mark in the ditch; there was only the impression of one footmark, and that was clearly made upon the grass. I did not undo the handkerchief containing the razor until the other men came up. Within a few days I had lent the prisoner's mother some money; she came to me on the Monday night; the day before the murder, and asked me to lend; she did not say it was for her; I lent her 10 shillings consisting of, as I believe, of two or three half-crowns, two shillings, and a sixpence. The spot at which I found the razor is close to the stile; any one passing the path to Salcot could not have put the razor into the ditch in the position in which I found it without stepping into the ditch. This was a common footpath.

By the Coroner. This prisoner's mother did not say what she wanted the money for? I have often lent her money before, and I think she had sometimes borrowed money for her son, although he has never asked me personally for any.

By the Jury: I last saw the prisoner after the murder before I found the razor, when he was taken by Beckwith at the public-house.

James Watling, cross-examined I was not in work but watching the coursing party; I saw Foakes find the handkerchief, and he had not touched it before I came up; I did not notice a footmark.

Mr. Church. Perhaps it was not very plain.

Witness I don't know.

John Wash said in cross-examination --- The inscription I spoke of on the razor was on top and not near the edge; the razor has been ground so many times that I can't trace any mark of it; I had used it for eight years, but had no particular mark on it, except that is was the heaviest razor I ever handled; the one produced is in every particular like mine; on the Sunday before the murder after I used the razor, I believe I placed the razor on the window sill near the road; this window is open to the garden and looks towards the road; there was a curtain to the window but the razor was not concealed by it; I very often put it there; it was in the case when I left it.

Re-examined by the Coroner. There is a small garden in front of the window, and I should think the distance from the garden to the road is about 11 or 12 feet; that window is usually kept shut, and has never been opened more than twice since I have been living in the house, which is two years last Michaelmas; of course I am only speaking as to my own knowledge; the window does open; Coats, my lodger, had a razor of his own, but his was not a very good one, and he occasionally shaved with mine; when I first came to Tollesbury I lodged with a man named Sheldrick, and his son, the present William Sheldrick, and the razor used to be about the house, so that he might at times have shaved with it, as it was a very good one and a great many persons used it; I never recollect seeing him use it.

By Mr. Church The prisoner to my knowledge carried a pig which had been recently killed; he brought it home from the butcher's, Mr. Anthony's, on Thursday before the murder, to my house; and about five weeks previously to that he had assisted in killing a pig for me; at Mr. Anthony's.

James Cobb, husband of the deceased, in cross-examination said --- When I did not use Wash's razor I used my own, but it has lately been out of repair; it is a black-handled razor, like the one produced, but there was nothing particular about it; a man named Coates, had lodged with me on the previous night but did not sleep with me on the night of the murder, because his boat was at Tollesbury; my other lodger left the house before I did; I had three razors altogether; I did not see what coin it was in the caddy, which was not taken. It was six o'clock when I left the house; before I went out I kissed mu wife; it was usual for me to do so nine mornings out of ten; three cottages are occupied by men, named Leaper, Ketchman, Wash and myself. I have not looked at my clothes, so that I don't know whether any are gone; I have missed nothing.

By the Coroner I had no share in the boat which the prisoner was about purchasing; if such a thing has been said it is not true.

After Abraham Foakes was examined and cross-examined, Abraham Emmery, thatcher, of Tollesbury was called to give evidence. On the morning of the murder the prisoner, Henry Harrington came to me at Young's beer-shop, at Salcot, where his father lodges; he came about a boat which he and I were going to purchase of Mr. Barton, at Wivenhoe; I paid £1 down for the boat about a months ago; we were to have it for £16.10, and to pay the remainder by instalments of 5s. a week between us; a third party was also concerned with us.

By Mr. Church: I am not aware of my own knowledge whether anything or money belonging to myself or lodgers was stolen; when I went out I left the door open, and the key inside; the back window of my cottage abuts upon an open school yard, out of which there is a swing gate opening into a footpath leading to the road.

Mary Wash, cross-examined by Mr. Church. The prisoner Harrington, slept at my house on the night before the murder; he got up about six, lighted a fire, had his breakfast and left about twenty minutes before seven; he did not come in again; he had on a plaid coat and drab trousers; a few days before he had carried some pork from Mr. Anthony's to my house; it was in a cloth, but I don't know whether he carried it on his back; he had also helped to kill a pig about five weeks previously; the cloth in which he brought home the dead pig was bloody, and I washed it; our coal shed is just close to the door of my cottage, so that it is a little public, but I do not think anyone could get anything out of it without my knowledge.

By the Coroner. My husband got up just before six o'clock, and left almost immediately to go to his work. Coates and his son also went to work I believe at the same time; the clock struck six while I was dressing, but I don't think I went down before half-past six; I did not go upstairs again for any purpose whatever till between 10 and 11 o'clock out of the house till I went to Cobb's cottage; my brother left the house just before I went downstairs; I did not see him, after he went out; he had on a dark plaid coat – the same one now produced; he wore the drab trousers now produced, and had them on for several days before this occurrence; I did not take any notice as to the spots on the trousers, and therefore I do not know that I should have observed them upon the trousers; he had three other old pairs of trousers, one of them in a dark tweed, the second a dark fustian, which had got rather light; by washing, and the other pair I believe were also fustian; I never observed spots of any kind upon any of them; I went across to Cobb's cottage about 8 o'clock; after that I was at home, and had the prisoner come home during the day I must have seen him; the window of the downstairs room has not been opened lately; I cannot say either where or when I saw my husband's razor last; I did not see it in the window sill when I came down in the morning; the last time I saw it my husband was using it on Sunday morning before the murder, but I don't know where he laid it afterwards; I don't know the razor if I see it; the prisoner the day before the murder, and had been employed some days previously; I cannot say anything as to what money he had about him.

By the Jury: I did not hear any noise downstairs that morning; I did not ask any question except as to what time it was; Mrs. Orrin came to my house about eight o'clock, and left just before I heard the child scream; Mrs. Orrin came back directly to Mrs. Raisin's gate, and I asked her what I should do, for I could not open Cobb's door; Mrs. Sampson came up to the door at the same time.

Cross-examined by Mr. Church The three pair of trousers belonging to the prisoner were found in the house the morning after the murder; he had three old coats besides the one he wore, and they were found in the house; two were tweeds, and the other the black one he has on; I don't recollect what coat the prisoner had on when he brought the part of the pig home; if the handkerchief belonging to the prisoner it had holes in it like the one produced I must have known it, and I am not aware that there were any holes in it; on Saturday morning last I found in my drawer downstairs a pink dotted handkerchief, pale, as I before said the prisoner's was; it was like the one produced, white ground dotted with pink, only much paler; the one found in the drawer is the prisoner's or at least the one I have washed for him; I am quite certain therefore, that this one found last week, and now produced, is not the prisoner's.

Mr. Church: Where is the handkerchief you found in the drawer?

Witness: Someone (I think the Superintendent of Police) took it.

Capt. Cook said he had not taken it; it was shown to him, but he did not remove it from the house.

By the Coroner: It was yesterday I placed the handkerchief on the table in my house, and while lying there Superintendent of Police, in company with another person, came in and I showed it them; as soon as they were gone from the house I missed the handkerchief.

By Mr. Church: I did not touch the body of the deceased or know whether it was cold or warm.

By the Coroner: The handkerchief I found in the drawer I had not seen before my examination on the last occasion.

By the Coroner. How come you looked for the handkerchief afterwards?

Witness: I don't know; I happened to put it in the drawer with my things, and found it when I looked into the drawer; I think it was the week before last I put the handkerchief in the drawer, together with some towels; it was covered up and not at the top of the drawer. That handkerchief I now swear to be the prisoner's. I am in the habit of washing linen for my brother, and my mother washed his trousers and other clothes; I can't say when the drab trousers were last washed.

The Coroner: Did you happen to look into the drawer before the last examination?

Witness: No, I found it quite accidentally, while looking for an apron; neither I, my husband, not any of my lodgers have a handkerchief like the one I found in the drawer; I placed the handkerchief in the drawer myself with some towels after washing them.

By the Jury: The drawers in which the handkerchief was found were in the lower room; I don't suppose anybody had been to the drawer between the last examination on Wednesday and the time I found the handkerchief; nobody had been into my house to stay except my mother, who came to me the day that my brother, (the prisoner) was taken, and remained with me that night; prisoner's father has not been to the house till today.

By the Coroner. When I found the handkerchief I mentioned it to my husband and his lodger, named Coates, and said I should not say anything about it, as I did not think it of consequence. The one produced before, with blood upon it, is not the prisoner's, and my reason for swearing that is that I have since found the one which I believe to be his in the drawer. If I had not found it, I should not have sworn positively to the other one being the prisoner's; there is no mark upon either of them. [The Coroner here called for the handkerchief and it was produced by Policeman Archer; the pattern, which is a very common one, is precisely the same as that of the handkerchief which had been with the razor; but it was, as the witness said, very much more faded, and indeed the pink spots were only just discernible.]

Policeman Archer examined. About one o'clock yesterday (Monday) I went with Supt. Cook to Wash's house, where the prisoner lodged. Supt. Cook asked Mrs. Wash how many handkerchiefs her brother, the prisoner, had; she said he had two, and that one of them, one of the blue ones, which Mr. Cook had taken away, belonged to him, and the other to her husband; that she had found the one belonging to the prisoner in a drawer, and upon that she opened the drawer and showed us the one produced, which is similar in size and pattern to the one which had been previously found in the ditch.; it was doubled up and appeared to have been recently washed and ironed; it was more faded than the one which has blood on it.

By the Jury. I had not heard any reports that a handkerchief had been found before I went to the house; I took it up and put it in my pocket; the handkerchief appeared to have been recently washed and ironed.

Cross-examined by Mr. Church. Two shirts belonging to the prisoner were immediately given up by Mrs. Wash on being asked for, as was also the handkerchief; I took the handkerchief unknown to my Superintendent, and had never up to the present time informed any one that I had it; it did not strike me as being an important piece of evidence, but intended to produce it here today if it were required; I can merely say that it struck me to be clean, and appeared as though recently ironed and folded.

The Coroner said it was somewhat singular that the witness did not at the examination, point out the circumstances of the prisoner's handkerchief having been so much more faded that the one she was called upon to speak to; and asked her why she had not on that occasion told the Jury that the spots on her brother's handkerchief were scarcely perceptible?

Witness replied that she did say then that it was much faded, but although she was in the habit of washing it she did not take particular notice of it.

The Coroner here observed that he understood a mallet and hedge stake had been found since the last examination; they had better now be produced. [They were accordingly placed upon the table. The former was a rudely-constructed instrument of some weight, and the latter an ordinary stake, made from an elm bough, broken at the middle, but not severed; about three feet in length and two inches perhaps in circumference.]

Mr Dawson, surgeon, deposed --- On Thursday last I examined the head of the deceased by dissection, assisted by Mr. Smyth and Mr. Tomlinson; from the state of the skin the blow must necessarily have been given previous to death; the upper portion of the temporal bone, which is very thin and brittle, is broken into ten or more fragments; I refer now more particularly to the blow upon the temple, which appeared to correspond with the hammer; I should not think such a blow would have produced immediate death --- it might have done, but I do not consider it probable; I have some doubts whether the fracture was occasioned by a blow from the hammer produced, because I think a blow from such a heavy instrument would have carried the fracture portions of the skull into the brain, although it is just possible that the blow may have been caused by a smart rap of the hammer; the other small wounds might have been produced by such an instrument as the claw of the hammer, but I think a blow from that would have injured the skull more; the hedge stake produced seems a very small instrument to produce such a fracture, although the appearance of the bark upon it corresponds with the bark on the window-sill of Cobb's house; at the time I saw that piece of bark which had been found there, I immediately said it was elm bark; the extremity of the yoke of the temporal bone was broken; several (five or six) more scratches on the face also afterwards became apparent.

The Coroner. Is it possible for the hedge stake to have caused such a fracture?

Mr. Dawson. It is possible; but the blow must have been given with great force from an instrument so light as this.

The Coroner. Asked whether Mr. Dawson had any fresh evidence to give respecting the wound in the throat, because there was at present a difference between his evidence already given upon that point and that given by Mr. Smyth, who was of opinion that from the jaggered nature of the wound it could not have been inflicted by so sharp an instrument as a razor? It was important that the medical testimony should be agreed upon this point.

Mr. Dawson said he had no reason to alter his previous opinion; the gash must have been cut with a razor, or some sharp instrument with a slightly convex edge.

The Coroner. In a wound of that description, how would the blood flow --- upwards? And do you think it possible for a party to inflict such a wound as that in the throat without covering his sleeves with blood?

Mr. Dawson. It is possible he may have done so, but not probable. Of course, the blood would naturally spurt up from the artery, although it might be intercepted by the jaw-bone; and this all depended upon whether the head was drawn back or not while the wound was being inflicted. If done with a razor, blood must undoubtedly have been left upon the hand of the party using it to control the razor he must have held it partly by the blade; but if the wound was caused by a long knife the hand would of course be further removed from the throat, and perhaps no blood would then reach the hand. There was no rupture of the brain.

Mr. Church. Is it your opinion that the wound that the poor woman received on the head killed her, or only produced insensibility?

Witness. Only rendered her insensible, I should say.

Mr. Church. And she might have remained so for a few hours afterwards?

Witness. Yes: or even a few days, supposing the wound in the throat had not been given.

Mr. Church. Upon the whole, then, is it your opinion that the blow on the head was produced by the hammer?

Mr. Dawson said it was a delicate question to give a positive opinion upon; if it were occasioned by the hammer there must have been several blows, or else a very smart tap must have been given. He thought, as he said before, that such a heavy instrument would have carried the skull in; his impression was rather that it was not caused by the hammer, but he did not say it was impossible that it could have been.

Mr. Church. Supposing the hedge stake to have been the instrument used, would not there have been marks of blood or hair left upon them?

Mr. Dawson. Under any circumstances there would have been no blood upon them, as the bruises had not penetrated through the skin; if deceased had her night cap on, as it is presumed she had, of course no hair would be left upon them, but if she had not there might have been. I don't think the mallet produced was the kind of instrument that could have inflicted the blow, and if it were done with the hedge stake it must have been a blow of great violence. The wound in the throat must have been produced by some instrument, whether a razor or knife, with a convex edge; of course, the fact of the razor having been found strengthened my opinion that the wound was inflicted with such an instrument; but my first impression on the subject was the same, and had it been the case of suicide I should have given the same opinion.

Mr. Church. Would not the party using the razor have run the risk of cutting himself?

Mr. Dawson. Ere was any struggling --- not without.

Mr. Church. Then is it your opinion that death was occasioned by the blow or the wound in the throat?

Mr. Dawson. I do not say which; death might have been produced by either, or conjointly.

Mr. Church. How long would it be in such a case before the body would get cold?

Mr. Dawson. Perhaps from four to six hours; but that would be regulated by the heat of the atmosphere and the quantity of bed clothes the deceased had over her.

Mr. Smyth, surgeon, who assisted Mr. Dawson in the examination of the head, said he agreed with that gentleman as to the appearances of it, and since giving his evidence on the last occasion he had again examined the cut in the throat, and did not see that he had any reason to alter the opinion he before gave. He supposed from the jagged appearance of the wound that it was not produced by so sharp an instrument as a razor, although he did not say it might not have been caused by such an instrument; he believed if the wound had been produced by a razor it would have been one complete cut; the jags he observed were upon the skin and not upon the flesh; he considered it possible that the wound might have been inflicted by the razor.

The Coroner. Is it possible that these jags might occur from the party holding the razor not being able to keep it steady?

Mr. Smyth. Certainly; it is very possible. The entire surface of the wound appeared to me to be uneven, but that still might have been occasioned by a razor; if you have an uneven cut on the outside you cannot have an even cut inside, because the same unsteadiness of the hand in using the instrument (assuming it to have been done so) might have occasioned the unevenness inside as well as outside.

The Coroner. Do you agree with Mr. Dawson as to the course of the flow of blood from such a wound?

Witness. Precisely; I also agree with him as to the probability of stains of the hands and clothes of the party inflicting the wound.

Cross-examined by Mr. Church. I should say the cause of death was the blow on the head and the cut conjointly. Insensibility I should think was first produced by the blow, and then of Course the cut expedited death. I believe deceased might have lived for hours or days under the effects of the blow, and that the cut in the throat alone would have occasioned death.

Mr. Church. Which of these instruments is the most likely to have occasioned the blows on the head?

Witness. I should say it was the hammer, certainly, or some other instrument. I don't think either of the other instruments could have affected it. No doubt more than one blow was given from the position which the wounds occupied.

Mr. Church. I believe you have considerable doubt whether the cut was inflicted by a razor?

Witness. The impression upon my mind was that it was not; but very possibly it might have been; of course, my previous opinion was in a measure shaken by the finding of the razor. The body of the deceased was warm when I first saw it, but the extremities were cold; it is impossible to give a positive opinion as to the length of time a body will remain warm; it all depends upon the temperature of the room, the quantity of bed clothes, and other circumstances. I understand the body of the deceased was warm till the afternoon. I should think deceased might have been dead about two hours when I saw her first. I should think it very improbable that the fracture on the head was produced by the hedge stake produced, because the depression in then scalp is perfectly circular; but I do not say it is not possible.

Policeman Charles Fox deposed --- On Saturday last, I found the hedge stake produced in an osier ground at the back of the deceased's house, broken as it now is. I then examined the hedge at the back of the house, and found a hole from which a hedge stake had been recently drawn. I fitted the stake to the hole and found it corresponded exactly. That was the first time the osier ground had been searched. The stake forms part of an elm bough, and on the morning of the murder I found on the window sill of the deceased's house a piece of bark precisely similar to that on the stake produced. I have not a piece of bark now, as I thought nothing of it at the time and did not keep it. I did not find any elm wood in the house of the deceased.

Cross-examined by Mr. Church. I found the stake directly opposite the back window of the cottage and about 25 yards distant from it. It is my opinion that the one produced is the stake which appeared to have been drawn from the hedge.

Elizabeth Orrin, widow, of Tollesbury, deposed --- I am a hawker, and about five minutes past eight on the morning of Tuesday, the 25th November, I went to the house of James Cobb to sell some tea; I found the door fastened, and thought Mrs. Cobb was out, for I had called many times before early in the morning, and never found the door fastened before; Mrs. Walsh said if I wanted her she would call her, but I said "No, I had two or three places to call at and I would call again; I then went away, and returned in about 40 minutes ; I tried the door twice again, and knocked loudly at it, when I heard the child crying, "Oh, my mother is dead—my mother is dead; " I then went to see if I could find any one in Ketchmaid's house to get something to break open the door, but not finding any one at home I returned immediately, and found Mrs. Wash with the key of the house.

Cross-examined. I am quite certain it was five minutes past eight when I first went to the door; I was away more than half an hour. Mr. Church said there was a discrepancy here as to time, for Mrs. Wash had said that it was eight o'clock when she heard the child cry. The witness, on re-examination, explained that she had when she first went to Mrs. Wash's told her that her clock was too slow; but to the best of her recollection it was 10 minutes to nine when she went a second time to Cobb's house.

Elijah Bowles examined --- I am a fish-merchant at Tollesbury; on the morning of the murder I met the prisoner, Henry Harrington, coming from the house out of the gate leading from his lodging: I had been in the habit of buying winkles off him, and asked him whether he had any to sell? He replied, " No; I'm turnipping (pulling turnips) now." I did not notice his dress particularly, but believe he had on a light fustian coat, and trousers of about the same material; he was coming up the street, which is the way to Salcot.

Prisoner. I called in at your house and got a pint of beer.

Cross-examined. The prisoner gave his answers in the usual manner; he walked slowly and did not seem in any degree flurried; he saw me coming when he left the gate; I would not swear to the coat he had on, but I believe it was not the one produced—it appeared much lighter; I cannot swear it is not the coat; prisoner had no weapon or stake in his hand.

Abraham Foakes, labourer, of Salcot. deposed—On Tuesday, the morning of the murder. about eight o'clock, I was at the bottom of the field next to Salcot Street, and saw Henry Harrington, the prisoner, coming through the foot-path going towards Salcot; I was about 40 rods from him ; he had on a dark plaid coat ; he passed me in the path, and I said "Morning, Henry," but he made no reply ; I had known the prisoner for some time ; as he did not speak to me, I thought he did not hear me, and nothing further passed; he then went on towards Salcot, and I left the field to go home a different way; he was then about 20 rods past the stile near which the razor was found ; he was walking rather quickly ; we generally spoke to each other when we met ; I spoke sufficiently loud for him to hear me ; he passed within half a rod of me, and I know he saw me, because he looked up just as he got by me; I was dressed as usual.

Abraham Emmery, thatcher, of Tollesbury. On the morning of the murder the prisoner, Henry Harrington, came to me at Young's beer-shop, at Salcot, where his father lodges; he came about a boat which he and I were going to purchase of Mr. Barton, at Wivenhoe ; I paid £1 down for the boat about a month ago; we were to have it for £16 10s, and to pay the remainder by instalments of 5s. a week between us; a third party was also concerned with us, but he said afterwards he would have nothing to do with it; this agreement was made five weeks back, so that the money due was 25s.; - no money was to be required of us till we got possession of the boat; we walked on to

Wivenhoe, and went to Mr. Barton's house about the boat, but he was not at home ; we waited about the quay for about a quarter of an hour or twenty minute; and then Harrington went to see Mr. Barton; I afterwards saw Mr. Barton, and told him the well of the boat was not deep enough, whereupon Mr. Barton said he would make it deeper; we went to the Ship at Launch public-house with Mr. Barton, who treated us to three pots of beer and bread and cheese, and we paid for two pots; I did not notice what money Harrington had about him, and whether he paid for his pot with a shilling or a half-crown I cannot say ; we returned to Salcot about seven in the evening, and stopped at Young's public-house, where we supped on some sprats which Harrington bought at Wivenhoe ; we went the same evening, about nine o'clock, to the Rising Sun, where I lodged, and he slept with me there; when he came to me on the Tuesday morning he had on the dark fustian coat now produced, and light fustian trousers; I did not notice that the trousers had any spots upon then; Beckwith, the policeman, came to the Rising Sun about nine o'clock, before we had finished our breakfast ; he told Harrington he was come after him concerning a murder; Harrington replied that he was ready and willing to go ; on the night previous to the murder I went to Tollesbury to talk to the prisoner about the boat; I asked him whether he was prepared to go to Wivenhoe, and how much money he got to go towards the boat; he told me 8s. 6d., but did not show it me; I returned to Salcot between three and four o'clock in the afternoon ; the prisoner was then pulling turnips; he had heard of a murder about seven o'clock on the Tuesday evening, the day on which it was committed ; it was talked about at the public-house, and Youngs told Harrington Fox was after him about it; we had heard who it was that was murdered, but, although it was close to Harrington's lodgings, no conversation took place between me and him on the subject of it; others in the room talked about it with him, but I don't know that I did in particular; I am first cousin to Harrington ; on our way to Wivenhoe Harrington went into the Lion, at Abberton; he said he had got a letter for a man (his cousin), and he went into that house to see if he were there every day, but hearing that he was not, he went on and put the letter in the post-office; on our way from Salcot to Wivenhoe we did not part company with the exception of that minute or two.

Cross-examined. When I first saw the prisoner on the Tuesday morning he did not appear to be flurried or agitated in his manner, nor did I observe any spots upon his trousers. Jeremiah Kelley was to have had a share in the boat; Cobb had nothing to do with it. When we returned to the beer-house the murder was the subject of general conversation; I do not remember the prisoner saying he wondered who had committed the murder. Prisoner did not seem at all agitated when Beckwith came to him, and he at once expressed his willingness to go with him. Fox had been to him the night before and searched him at the Rising Sun.

James Jenkins, beer-shop keeper, of Wivenhoe, deposed—On Tuesday, the 25th inst. the prisoner came to my beer-house at Wivenhoe alone and had a pint of beer; he gave me half a crown to pay for it, and I gave him the change. I did not observe anything particular about him; he did not stop two minutes, but took his change and went out.

Cross-examined. Prisoner sat down in the tap-room for two minutes; I did not observe anything remarkable about him; he seemed a roughish chap, and nipped the beer into him and cut off. (Laughter.)

Mary Ann Wenlock, servant to Mr. Chamberlain, of the Ship at Launch, Wivenhoe, examined. The prisoner came into the Ship at Launch shortly after two o'clock in the afternoon of Tuesday, the 25th inst., and had two pots of porter; he gave me in payment a half-crown, and I gave him 1s. 10d. change. I had never seen the prisoner before nor since till today.

Charles Last, miller, of Salcot, deposed—On Tuesday night I was in the Rising Sun, Salcot, and saw Harrington there; Emmery, Wood, and several others were present. There was some conversation in the tap-room about the murder, and I heard Harrington say, "It appears impossible to me that anyone could have gone up and murdered the woman without waking the child, as the child laid only two feet from the bed." I had not heard anything about a child mentioned before that; and the prisoner said, " Perhaps that might be about it". Soon after Harrington left the room to go to bed.

Cross-examined. Very little was said in the room about the murder; it had been talked about a good deal in the street; I don't know that it had been said in the street that the woman was lying in bed with her throat cut, nor that anything was said as to the position of the child. Wood, who was in the room, made the observation that the child was only a step from the bed; I did not hear anyone say before Harrington spoke that the child was lying two feet from the bed. The matter might have been talked of good deal in the village, but I had not heard it.

Jas. Digby, bricklayer's labourer, examined. I know Henry Harrington, the prisoner; last winter or last spring time, I can't say which, I and Harrington were winkling together; he was speaking concerning Mrs. Cobb, the deceased, and said that she had been saying something about him, and that she should not tell any lies about him, for if she did he would give her a ' putting up; " or an expression to that effect; I don't know that he was altogether angry at the time; about a year ago I lodged at Cobb's house, and had been occasionally shaved by Cobb with Wash's razor; it was a large razor with black handle, and was generally kept in a black case; both the case and razor produced are very much like the one, and that is all I can say.

Cross-examined. I don't recollect exactly what words the prisoner used when he spoke about Mrs. Cobb; I considered he meant to give her a blowing up.

William Sheldrake, mariner, of Tollesbury, with whose father the witness John Wash had lodged four or five years ago, was called to prove the identity of the razor, but it appeared that he had not seen it for so long a period as to render him unable to give any satisfactory evidence, and his examination was not continued.

William Beckwith, parish constable of Tollesbury, examined. About ten o'clock on Tuesday last I heard that Mrs. Cobb had been murdered, and in the course of the same day I heard that the prisoner was suspected, and that policeman Fox was gone after him; on the following morning I had occasion to go to Colchester, and when I got to Salcot, which was on my way, I went into the Rising Sun. where I found the prisoner eating some victuals; Emmery was sitting alongside of him; I told the prisoner I wanted him to go to Tollesbury with me, and he said he was ready to go as soon as I was; Harrington, Emmery, and the landlord (Edward Young) were talking about the murder, and as soon as I went in they dropped the subject: I then brought him on to Tollesbury, but no conversation took place on the way about the murder; I took the prisoner to my house, where I met Fox and the other police, and gave him into the custody of the former; the prisoner had on it dark plaid coat and light fustian trousers; as he turned round from the fire upon lighting his pipe I observed some spots, apparently of ink, on the right leg of his trousers; the spots were quite white all round them, and appeared to me to have been fresh done over with white chalk; when I got him to my house I asked him what the spots were, but the prisoner made no reply.

Cross-examined. The murder was the subject of much conversation throughout Tollesbury, and I dare say it was known throughout Salcot, the adjacent village; general wonder was expressed in the parish that the murder could have been committed with the child lying so near to the woman's bed; when I went to the prisoner he did not betray any signs of fear, and walked quietly with we to Tollesbury without handcuffs; I believe the marks on the trousers to be ink, and the white round them appeared very much like chalk. [The prisoner's trousers were here produced for the inspection of the Coroner and Jury. In addition to the ink spots already described there appeared to be several faint smears of red, apparently of blood, in several parts of the trousers.]

Policeman Fox examined. On Tuesday evening last, from information I received, I went to the Sun public-house and inquired for the prisoner, upon which Harrington called out " Here am I." I obtained a candle and took the prisoner into another room, where I asked him to strip; he took off some of his clothes, and I examined his shirt and shirt sleeves, but found no traces of blood upon them; the shirt sleeves were short. I then examined the trousers, and found the hind part of the left leg, about the seat. and the fore part of the right leg, covered with slud; I asked him how his trousers came all over mud on both sides? He said it was from slipping from the sea wall. I then said it was very curious that both sides should be dirtied in once slipping down; the prisoner said. " I suppose you are examining me on account of the murder:" I asked him what time he left Tollesbury that morning? He said " Seven, or a little before seven." I asked him whether he saw any one as he came away from his house? and he replied, " No, I did not." I then told him he must be at the King's Head to attend the inquest the next day at eleven o'clock; He said, "Me and Emmery are coming up to Tollesbury tomorrow, and I will be sure to be at the King's Head, or at home, at 10 o'clock." On the following morning I was at Beckwith's, when he brought the prisoner, and I took him into custody on the charge of murder; on looking at the prisoner's trousers I then observed spots something like ink where the previous night I had seen mud; the trousers appeared to have been rubbed a good deal where the ink was, and I also observed red marks, as if of blood, both above and below the knee; I called his attention to the marks, and the prisoner said he knew nothing about them ; when standing out of Beckwith's house the prisoner said, " I carried a pig's pluck, and the blood might have dropped off of that."

Cross-examined. When I found the prisoner at the public-house at Salcot he told me that he heard I was coming there after him, and that he waited there for me ; the mud was upon the prisoner's trousers on the right and left seat, and both before and behind on the right leg; I found 1s 5d upon the prisoner ; the prisoner said he carried a pig's pluck, but did not mention the name of Anthony; the prisoner exhibited no fear, trepidation, or confusion while I was searching him, and in fact his conduct was rather that of an innocent man.

Captain Charles Cook, Superintendent of Police at Witham, deposed—On the morning of Wednesday last, the day after the murder, I received the prisoner into my custody from Policeman Fox; I took him to the Plough and Sail Inn, Tollesbury, where I examined the prisoner's trousers; I observed some spots on the right thigh, in font, and while I was examining them the prisoner said " I don't know how that came there: I carried home some pig's pluck not long ago; I am innocent, I know". On the same day I searched the prisoner's lodgings, and in the bed in which I was informed he slept I found two coats, two waistcoats, two pairs of trousers, two blue pocket handkerchiefs, one neckerchief, and a clean shirt ; these were stated by Mrs. Wash as being all the things the prisoner had in the house; one of the blue handkerchiefs she has since told me belonged to her husband : I did not search the drawers, because Mrs. Wash told me the prisoner had nothing else in the house belonging to him; I produce the jacket worn by the prisoner when he was apprehended; upon the lining of the right hand pocket I find a red smear, apparently of blood; one pair of trousers taken from the prisoner's bed was stained on the lining of the right hand pocket with two large spots of red, apparently blood, and the hind part of the right leg also bears similar marks; the blood on the pocket had gone through the lining and stained the flap; Upon the lining of the right hand pocket in one of the jackets there is also a red mark, as though of blood; the razor and handkerchief produced I received from Mr. Dawson on Wednesday afternoon, after the inquest, in the same state as they are now.

Cross-examined. I cannot undertake to say that the faint stain in the pocket of the coat taken from the prisoner is blood, or that it is of recent date; I found no other stains resembling blood on the coat; I cannot undertake to say that the stains found upon the other article of clothing taken from the prisoner's house are those of blood; the stains upon the lining of the trousers pocket, found at the prisoner's lodgings, appeared to be of recent date, as the spots were stiff, as if the clothes had not been used; I suppose they might have been there three weeks or upwards; prisoner said he had been carrying a pig's pluck not long before, but did not say anything about Mr. Anthony.

Mr. Dawson, being re-called, proved that he received the razor and handkerchief produced from the witness Foakes, and handed them over shortly afterwards to Supt. Cook.

William Elijah Walford, of Wivenhoe, cordwainer, examined. On Tuesday, the 25th ultimo. I saw the prisoner at the Ship at Launch public-house, about three o'clock; he came and sat against me, and told me " If I can get a berth, I will go to sea; I don't like the idea of working upon the land for sixteen pence per day; " he soon after left the house.

Cross-examined. I mentioned this statement of the prisoner to Mr. Barton, and through him it came to the knowledge of the police; nothing more passed from the prisoner than that which I have stated.

Policeman Archer, being re-called, said—On Wednesday last I received the prisoner into my custody at the Plough and Sail, from policeman Fox, together with a pair of trousers marked with black spots; after I had removed them, prisoner said " I am innocent. I don't know how the blood came upon them trousers, unless I got it of the ropes on board;" previous to this, the word blood had not been mentioned. It being now nearly ten o'clock, the Coroner here said it would be utterly impossible to conclude the inquiry that night, because in addition to the time that would necessarily be occupied in summing up the evidence, an opportunity must be afforded for investigating further the circumstances attending the production of the second handkerchief, as to which the evidence was at present very unsatisfactory.

A Juryman (Mr. Solly) asked whether it was in contemplation to send the prisoner's clothes to Professor Taylor, with a view to ascertain whether the stains upon them were those of blood?

The Coroner said it was not proposed to do so, inasmuch as it was impossible to distinguish by chemical analysis animal from human blood, nor was it possible to ascertain how long the blood might have been on any of the articles of clothing.

A Juryman said it would not, at all events, be necessary to send all the prisoner's clothes upon which stains had been found, because it was not probable that he wore that morning all the pairs of trousers found at his lodgings, each of which bore more or less marks of that description.

The Coroner said it would be a question for the consideration of the Jury which of the clothes the prisoner wore. Some conversation took place as to the day most convenient for closing the inquiry, in the course of which Captain Mc Hardy intimated that it was desirable to do so without delay, inasmuch as the prisoner (the Coroner having no power to detain him during the interval of adjournment) was now under remand by the magistrates to appear before them on Thursday, when it was possible, if the Jury had not come to a decision, they might deem it advisable to go into the charge against him.

Mr. Church said there would be no necessity for that, as it was constantly the practice of magistrates in the metropolis and elsewhere to extend the period of remand from time to time until the Coroner's Jury had found a verdict.

The Coroner afterwards said he now understood there would not be, in all probability, any other evidence forthcoming upon the subject of the additional handkerchief found by the prisoner's mother. About ten o'clock the inquest was adjourned till the following day.—At the close of the proceedings there was a general rush on the part of those assembled to obtain a parting glance at the prisoner, who, by permission of Capt. Mc Hardy, afterwards had an interview with his mother.

THIRD DAY --- WEDNESDAY

The inquiry was resumed at twelve o'clock on Wednesday morning, when

Elizabeth Wash, wife of Chas. Wash, dredgerman, of Tollesbury, deposed—On Tuesday, the day of the murder, I was at the cottage of John Wash, where Henry Harrington lodged; in the afternoon Mrs. Wash opened the drawer and said, "I wonder where John's (meaning her husband's) razor is," adding. " I dare say he has put it up somewhere, but I don't know ;" she did not find the razor while I was there—at least I did not see it. Mrs. Wash was washing, and I cannot tell what caused her to look into the drawer.

By the Jury. I don't remember that Mrs. Wash looked on to the window sill for the razor; I mentioned this circumstance to Mrs. Heard soon afterwards, but did not think anything of it. I am often in at Mrs. Wash's, but never observed the razor on the sill, and I don't know that I ever saw the razor in my life.

Mrs. Wash, being re-called, said—I think I last washed the handkerchief which I found in the drawer on Saturday, the week before Henry was taken; I mentioned that I had found the handkerchief to my husband and Coates, our lodger. I did not think it worthwhile to mention it to anyone else, as I thought it would not signify --- I thought that would not "add nor diminish" anything. The witness Elizabeth Wash, who is related to me, was at my house on the day of the murder; I recollect I said in the course of the day. "I wonder where my husband's razor is;" I looked in the window-sill and then on the drawers, but could not find the razor; I don't recollect that I opened the drawer to look for it at all; my husband kept it in so many places that I never knew where to find it.

The Coroner. Then that is just the reason which should have induced you to look all over the house for it.

Witness. Well, I should not have thought about it only they were talking about Cobb's razors.

One of the Jury expressed his belief that the witness had before stated that she had never looked for the razor at all.

Mrs. Wash said she did not remember saying so. It was not in the same drawer from which I took the handkerchief that I looked for the razor—we never kept any linen in it. I have frequently seen my husband put the razor in the drawer, and sometimes in the cupboard; I don't recollect that I looked in those places.

The Coroner. Although you had been wondering where your husband had put the razor, it did not occur to you to look for it in either of these places?

Witness. No, because I did not take any heed of it.

By the Jury. I never had a handkerchief of this pattern in the house belonging to either myself or husband; it is a very common pattern.

By the Coroner. My clock at the time of the murder was half an hour slower than the Church clock.

A Juryman explained that it was customary in Tollesbury to keep the church clock about half an hour too fast. This concluded the examination of witnesses, and

The Coroner then proceeded to sum up the evidence, observing that it would now be his duty to go through the whole of the facts adduced before them on this painful occasion, and must request, and had no doubt they would devote, their best attention and consideration to them. The cause of the death of this unfortunate woman was too palpable and apparent to admit of any doubt that she had been brutally murdered by someone; and the question for their consideration now was whether all the facts and circumstances elicited before them were sufficient to lead them to the conclusion that Henry Harrington, the man now suspected and in custody, was the guilty party. He then read through the whole of the depositions, pointing out and commenting upon such parts of them as bore materially upon the charge against the prisoner. Crimes of this magnitude (he observed) were seldom established by direct and positive testimony; but were usually brought home to the guilty party by what was termed circumstantial evidence, or a combination of circumstances which naturally and usually attend such a crime. They would have to say whether in this case the circumstances were sufficient to satisfy their minds that Henry Harrington, the man suspected, was the guilty party ; and if they could come to no conclusion than that he was really the party who committed this crime, it would be their duty to return a verdict of wilful murder against him ; but if, on the other hand, they entertained a doubt—and it must be a reasonable doubt—they would then find a verdict of wilful murder against some person or persons unknown. The room was here cleared, and the Jury were in deliberation about half-an-hour. On re-admission

The Foreman announced the verdict of the Jury to be ---

" WILFUL MURDER against Henry Harrington." The Coroner then issued his warrant for the committal of the prisoner to take his trial at the Spring Assize. The inquiry terminated soon after three o'clock. The interest manifested on Tuesday had considerably abated towards the close of the investigation, owing probably to the absence of the prisoner, whose presence was not deemed necessary, nor was his professional adviser in attendance on Wednesday.

From the *Norfolk Chronicle*, Saturday, December 1851 a report about the committal and about the adopted girl in the bedroom at the time of the murder.

The Tollesbury Murder. —The prisoner Henry Harrington was examined in Witham, on Friday last, and again remanded. He appeared but little concerned with his awful situation. In the course of Friday afternoon Inspector Cooke proceeded to Tollesbury to make some important inquiries concerning the clothing which the prisoner wore on the morning of the murder; and we are informed that such facts were elicited as will tend to clear up considerably the mystery which overhangs the tragical affair. Spots of blood are traced on his trowsers, and in or near the pocket a kind of browns flock coat which he had on when captured. In his statement to the coroner he observed that he wore the same coat on Tuesday morning, but as the sleeves did not exhibit the least signs of blood, his story was doubted, as it was deemed almost impossible for a murder like that committed upon the unfortunate woman to have been perpetrated without staining the assailant's hands, arms with blood. The mystery has been cleared up, however, and the police we are instructed, have succeeded in finding a jacket, which, in all probability, will be found to have been worn by the prisoner on the morning in question. The escape of the little girl, who slept in the crib by the side of the bedstead of the unfortunate woman, has been the subject of much observation throughout the district. She is an interesting child, between six and seven years of age, and had been adopted by the poor creature and her husband. Had the child awoke at the moment of the villain committing the diabolical deed there is little doubt that she would have shared the same fate as her protectress. The murdered woman bore a very excellent character in the village, and the comfortable, clean and respectable appearance of the interior of the cottage, excited attention when it was visited by the coroner and jury[15].

A snippet about a candle appeared in the *Chelmsford Chronicle* the following week.

We understand that a piece of candle has been found trodden underfoot in the room of the deceased, and a piece was missing from one of the candlesticks, which leads to the intrigue that the murder was committed at an early hour. As an illustration of the feeling shown by parties in the matter, it may be mentioned that Wash has inquired if he shall get his razor back, as he says, "it is a good bit of stuff."[16]

---

[15] *Norfolk Chronicle*, Saturday 6th December 1851

[16] *Chelmsford Chronicle*, Friday 12th December 1851

4. Changing Victorian Attitude to Capital Punishment

During the earlier part of the century, attitudes were altered towards the subject of capital punishment. In Parliament, reformers attempted to change the law to remove capital punishment. Mr William Ewart, MP (1798 – 1869), attempted to introduce a Bill to Parliament on 14th March 1848 under the title 'Punishment of Death' with the sole aim of having capital punishment abolished in the UK. He claimed that there had been a change in attitudes by 'many magistrates, many clergymen [and that] among the mass of the people generally, in society itself, the feeling against capital punishment is more widely spread'[17]. However, opposing the motion the Home Secretary, Sir George Grey MP (1799 – 1882) convinced the House that it would not be in the interests of the country to abolish capital punishment for all offences. He even hinted that had Ewart kept the punishment for treason and other similar offences, he might have been in favour of some form of abolition.

Ewart's premise was also based on the practice that some Juries had now adopted in murder capital cases, whereby they preferred to excuse the defendants rather than send them to their deaths. This tide of both moral and theological affinity towards more humane treatment of criminals gained momentum as the decade came to an end. One critic of capital punishment was Charles Dickens, who wrote to the London Times the following letter[18]:

---

[17] http://hansard.millbanksystems.com/commons/1848/mar/14/punishment-of-death#S3V0097P0_18480314_HOC_20 [Accessed 10th May 2017]

[18] Charles Dickens, 'Letter to the Editor', *The Times*, 13th November 1849

MR. CHARLES DICKENS AND THE EXECUTION OF THE MANNINGS.

Mr. EDITOR, --- I was a witness of the execution at Horsemonger-Lane. I went there with the intention of observing the crowd gathered to behold it, and I had excellent opportunities of doing so, at intervals all through the night, and continuously from daybreak until after the spectacle was over. I do not address you on the subject with any intention of discussing the abstract question of capital punishment, or any of the arguments of its opponents or advocates. I simply wish to turn this dreadful experience to some account for the general good, by taking the readiest and most public means of advertising to an intimation given by Sir G. Grey in the last Session of Parliament, that the Government might be induced to give its support to a measure making the infliction of capital punishment a private solemnity within the prison walls (with such guarantee for the last sentence of the law being inexorably and surely administered as should be satisfactory to the public at large), and of most earnestly beseeching Sir G. Grey, as a solemn duty which he owes to society, and a responsibility which he cannot forever put away, to originate such legislative change himself.

I believe that a sight so inconceivably awful as the wickedness and levity of the immense crowd collected at that execution could be imagined by no man, and could be presented in no heathen land under the sun. The horrors of the gibbet and of the crime which brought the wretched murderers to it, faded in my mind before the atrocious bearing, looks and language, of the assembled spectators. When I came upon the scene at midnight, the *shrillness* of the cries and howls that were raised from time to time, denoting that they came from a concourse of boys and girls already assembled in the best places, made my blood run cold. As the night went on, screeching and laughing, and yelling in strong chorus of parodies on negro melodies, with substitution of 'Mrs Manning' for 'Susannah', and the like, were added to these. When the day dawned, thieves, low prostitutes, ruffian and vagabonds of every kind, flocked on to the ground, with every variety of offensive and foul behaviour. Fightings, faintings, whistlings, imitations of Punch, brutal jokes, tumultuous demonstrations of indecent delight when swooning women were dragged out of the crowd by police with their dresses disordered, gave a new zest to the general entertainment. When the sun rose brightly --- as it did --- it gilded thousands upon thousands of upturned faces, so inexpressibly odious in their brutal mirth and callousness, that a man had cause to feel ashamed of the shape he wore, and to shrink from himself, as fashioned in the image of the Devil. When the two miserable creatures who attracted all this ghastly sight about them were turned quivering into the air, there was no more emotion, no more pity, no more thought that two immortal souls had gone to judgement, no more restraint in any of the previous obscenities, than if the name Christ had never been heard in this world, and there was no belief among men but that they perished like the beasts. I have seen, habitually, some of the worst sources of general contamination and corruption in this country, and I think there are not many phases of London life that could surprise me. I am solemnly convinced that nothing that ingenuity could devise to be done in this city, in the same compass of time, could work such ruin as one public execution, and I stand astounded and appalled by the wickedness it exhibits. I do believe that any community can prosper where such a scene of horror and demoralisation as was enacted outside Horsemonger-Lane Jail is presented at the very doors of good citizens, and is passed by, unknown or forgotten. Any when, in our prayers and thanksgivings for the season, we are humbly expressing before God our desire to remove the moral evils of the land, I would ask your readers to consider whether it is not a time to think of this one, and to root it out.

    I am, Sir, your faithful servant,

           Charles Dickens,

Devonshire-Terrace, Tuesday Nov, 13.

This letter was reproduced over the next few weeks in many publications from the *Evening Standard* and *The Era* to provincial newspapers, such was the interest in the subject matter.

Whereas Dickens stated that he did not wish to argue against capital punishment, it is clear that his distaste for the spectacle of public execution also exposes his uneasiness with the whole barbaric nature of taking lives in such an industrial manner. Dickens was just one of many well-known Victorian reformers seeking a change, but this is not to say the Victorians were easy on crime. They were not, and were very concerned about the levels of crime in their society. However, there remained a dissatisfaction with the spectacle of public executions.

On 1st December 1849 Ewart again brought forward a Bill, this time titled 'Abolition of the Punishment of Death'[19]. His evidence this time, was based on an increase in the number of murders up and down the country. It was a 'lamentable' increase, Ewart stated, and was he not correct in bringing forward such a Bill, since the death penalty had not deterred murderers carrying out their crimes. He also maintained that 'it was most justly considered by the public that these degrading exhibitions [hangings] contaminated public morality, just as Dickens had argued.

Sir George Grey, again opposed the motion, again claiming that 'the time is yet far distant when we can safely dispense with the extreme penalty of the law in cases of extreme guilt'.

This time the 'Ayes' numbered 51 and the 'Noes' 75, again rejecting any change in the law.

The law remained essentially unchanged for another century of course, but the awareness to the spectacle of public executions did eventually have them removed to within the walls of the prison by the end of 1868 and out of public sight. All this though, would not help Henry Harrington in evading the death penalty, should the Jury

---

[19] http://hansard.millbanksystems.com/commons/1849/may/01/abolition-of-the-punishment-of-death#S3V0104P0_18490501_HOC_16 [Accessed 16th may 2017]

find him guilty. As will be seen from his trial below, even the prosecution refers to state of the law on capital punishment, and the growing uneasiness that had, according to the lawyer, changed the verdicts on several murder cases in the recent past, suggesting that murderers had been spared the death penalty by being found not guilty when they should really have been executed for their crimes. As will be seen, the prosecution disapproved of such acts of 'tolerance' towards offenders and made sure the jury were armed with this information.

5 The Trial

The next time the case is mentioned is when it came to court in March 1852. The *Chelmsford Chronicle* had the full proceeding report, but the quality was not good. It was repeated by the *Essex Standard* on Friday 5th and 12th March 1852:

The Tollesbury Murder

The trial of Henry Harrington charged with the wilful murder of Elisabeth Cobb at Tollesbury, having been fixed for yesterday morning, long before the hour for formally opening the Court a crowd of persons besieged the doors anxious to obtain admittance, although the excitement bore no comparison with that which prevailed upon the trial of Drory at the Lent Assize of last year, owing probably to a rumour which had prevailed that an application would be made for the postponement of the trial, in consequence of the illness of a material witness. The Court however, was densely crowded, and upon the bench we observed the Hon. Mrs. Mildmay and Rev. C.A. St John Mildmay, the lady of T.W. Bramston, Esq. and Miss Bramston, Rev. W. Hulland, &c., &c.

The case for the prosecution was conducted by Mr. Bodkin and Mr. Rodwell; and the prisoner was defended by Mr. Parry and Mr. Woolett, upon the joint instructions of Mr. J.H. Church, of Colchester, and Mr. Durrent, of Chelmsford.

The Jury were composed of the following parties: - Mr. C. Hones, Mr. Thomas Brooks, Mr. Thomas Everitt, Mr. John Filer, Mr. Charles Foster, Mr. Thomas Jolly, Mr. John Kidney, Mr. W. Parsons, Mr. Nathaniel Stone, Mr. Samuel Thorne, Mr. Nathaniel Filer, and Mr. James Ward.

At the request of Mr. Parry the witnesses to be examined were ordered out of court till required to give evidence.

Mr. Bodkin, in opening the case for the prosecution, said the case before them was one of the highest character which could possibly occupy the attention of any tribunal. The prisoner was charged with the wilful murder of the unfortunate woman whose name they had heard from the indictment, and under circumstances which justified him in bespeaking that which he was sure they would not refuse him --- a patient attention to the circumstances connected with this charge, which he would proceed, as shortly as was consistent with his duty, and as clearly as he was able to do, to lay before them in such an order as to enable them to understand the evidence, and to apply it when the witnesses were brought before them. The person about whose unhappy death they were now about to enquire was the wife of a person named Cobb, employed on the water as a dredgerman, and living of Tollesbury. The deceased and her husband lived together upon terms of affection and happiness, consistent with their station in life; the former was about 33 years of age, and had no family of her own, but, actuated by that maternal affection which women frequently showed, having no offspring of her own, she had adopted a child of the name of Spurgin, six years of age, who was sleeping in her room at the time of her death. There lived also in the cottage tow lodgers of the name of Mason and Pewter, both following the same occupation of dredgerman, and the two upper rooms were usually occupied, one of them by those lodgers, and the other by Cobb, his wife, and the little child, who slept in a small crib at a little distance from their bed. On the morning of Tuesday, the 25th of November, Cobb and Mason left the cottage about quarter past six o'clock (Pewter having slept away from home that night, to follow their occupation on the water), leaving his wife in bed in the enjoyment of perfect health, and the child sleeping in the crib before alluded to; and both men were engaged at work together when the fatal news of the barbarous murder of the unfortunate wife reached them. James Cobb went from the house soon after six o'clock; he left the door latched, so that any person could have access through it to the upstairs rooms. A little before eight o'clock a woman, named Elizabeth Orrin, a tea-hawker, who had been in the habit of calling at the cottage, tried the door and found it fastened, upon which she left for about three-quarters of an hour; she then returned and, finding the door still locked, she struck it several times so as to arouse the child upstairs, who screamed violently saying that her mother was dead. Mrs. Orrin gave an alarm to some neighbours, who obtained the key from the child through the window, and on getting upstairs a most lamentable scene presented itself, the poor woman being found in bed with her throat cut, and some severe blows inflicted on the skull, which was fractured into 16 or 17 pieces. The clothes from boxes, in that and the adjoining room were scattered about the floor, and from a till in one of them a small sum of money, amounting to about 12s., had been taken away; so that he thought there would be no obscurity either as to the cause or mode of the deceased's death, the time at which the murder was committed, nor would there be any as to the trifling and very inadequate object induced some person or other to commit this atrocious deed. The learned gentleman then detailed the leading features of the case as bearing against the prisoner --- mentioning the fact of his being the only male person left near the cottage after the dredgermen had gone to their work, and alluding to an untruth which he subsequently told respecting the time he left for Salcot on the morning of the murder; the discovery of the razor and the handkerchief in the woolve in the pathway which the prisoner was seen to pass on his way to Salcot; the blood partially affected by ink on his trousers, and the fact of his having spent money subsequent to the murder, although he was known to be in very straitened circumstances a few days previously, were also noticed at some length. In conclusion the learned gentleman observed that the present inquiry was conducted in public grounds for the security of the public and the safety of society. He was rejoiced to find that the prisoner had been fortunate enough to obtain the assistance of his friends here to defend him; and he was sure it must be a matter of congratulations to all of them to know that, if the law must remove from the face of the earth a being who had committed such an offence as this, it would not take its course of just vengeance without the aid of the prisoner of the best talent and ability which could be procured for him. His friend, in the defence, would probably deal with the acts proved for the prosecution of themselves little and unimportant; but it would be their duty, in forming their conclusion, to deal with the whole combination of small circumstances, and if, after a calm and dispassionate inquiry into all the facts connected with the charge, they could see such a reasonable doubt as in the ordinary transactions of life they would feel it their duty to give effect to, then the prisoner was entitled to ask at their hands the benefit of that doubt; but if, on the other hand, under the circumstances – all of them verging from one point --- brought them to the irresistible conclusion that the man at the bar did commit the offence which the indictment imputed to him --- then, however painful their duty, they would not hesitate to discharge that duty upon which, in the face of the country, they on their solemn oaths had pledged themselves to.

James Cobb, husband of the deceased, examined by Mr. Rodwell

On the night of the 24th Nov. I went to bed about nine o'clock; Wm. Mason, myself, and wife, and Eliza Spurgin (a child about seven years of age whom I had adopted) slept in the house that night; another dredgerman named Pewter was away from home. The child slept in a crib about two feet from the bed; on the morning of the 25th of Nov. I got up at a quarter before six, and left my wife lying in bed; she asked me what time I should be at home, and I told her half-past one, when I went downstairs Mason came in from the garden belonging to me and the other cottages, and took his jacket, and went off to his work; John Wash, who lives in the cottage opposite mine, who went to his work on the water, and I followed him about ten minutes past six; I latched the door only, and left the key inside as usual; the casement window of the ground floor room opens onto garden, which looks into the school yard, and was fastened inside when I left the house; it was large enough to take the body of a man; I then went to my work at the river about two miles off, and found there John Wash, Coates and his son, but did not see Mason; I got home from my work between two and three o'clock, and found my wife in bed, with her throat cut; she was in a different position to that in which I left her; lying upon her left side; nearly all the contents of my clothes box were emptied out on the floor, but a tea-caddy on the drawers, in which I had some money, had not been touched; I never recollect seeing the prisoner in my house but once, and that was about a month before the murder; when he came to bring some flat fish from his sister, Mrs. Wash; I had been just before looking at a boat, which, however, I did not buy, and it was sold for £9; it was well known all over the place that I had been after buying the boat; I found a small piece of elm bark and a piece of leaf on the window-sill leading to the garden, but I have not preserved it.

Cross-examined by Mr. Parry. The prisoner had not been in the habit of visiting me; there are two cottages adjoining that of Wash, occupied by Hesikah Ketchmaid, a man named Lowper and his two sons, and Argent Bultoo, there was a hedge stake found in an ozier bed about 5 rods at the back of the cottage[20].

Mr. Frederick Chancellor, of Chelmsford, proved the accuracy of the plan showing the premises at which the murder took place, the road to Salcot, &c., --- In cross-examination of the witness explained the position at which the hedge stake was found, which was in exactly contrary direction from the road to Salcot.

Cobb, in further examination said --- My clock was half an hour too fast; Mason had left the house about three minutes before I did; I overtook some men on my way to work, but not my mates; there are a great many cottages near me principally occupied by dredgermen; I think I got aboard my boat about seven; I did not hear of my wife's death till I was within a quarter of a mile from my house; I met Mr. Solly and he said to me, "Do you know what we are upon?" I answered "No, sir; is my wife murdered?" I did not say that before Mr. Solly and Mr. Seachurch had told me of it that know of, but I had been questioned by the policeman all the way coming from my boat about my razors, and that's what made me suppose that she was murdered; I had used Wash's razor on and off for a year and a half, and my lodgers have been shaved with it as well as myself; I have been sentenced to seven years transportation for taking oysters in Burnham river.

---

[20] 1 rod = 5.02 metres

Re-examined. At the expiration of four years of my sentence I returned to my home and married my late wife, with whom I always lived very happily.

William Mason, dredgerman, of Tollesbury, who said he had lodged with Cobb for two years and a half previously to this occurrence, corroborated his evidence as to the time if their leaving the house on the morning of the murder; in a till in a box upstairs he had 12s., including two half crowns, which was taken, and all his clothes were turned out of the same box. He got home from his work about two o'clock and found his things in this state of confusion and his money gone; the money he had saved up and put it in his box at different times, but he could swear that there were amongst the silver two half crowns.

Cross-examined by Mr. Parry. I cannot tell exactly what time it was I left the cottage, but I should think it was not quite so late as half past six o'clock; I had no particular time to get to work; I have not that I know of said that it was about half past six when I left Cobb's house; but it was sometime between six and seven.

Edward Pewter, another lodger of Cobb's, proved that he left Cobb's house on the Monday night before the murder and went on board a smack at Woodrup[21], near Tollesbury, and kept out fishing until the Wednesday, when he was at home he slept in the same room with Mason; witness's clothes were all thrown out of his box when he got back to Cobb's about midday on the Wednesday; Cobb and his wife seemed very happy together, and during the eleven months he had been there he had never heard an angry word between them.

Cross-examined, Cobb used to shave me with Wash's razor; and, was in the habit of setting it for him.

Mr. Solly, farmer, of Tollesbury, deposed that about noon on the day of the murder he went on board the smack in which Cobb was engaged, for the purpose of telling him of the murder. Did not recollect Cobb asking any question about his wife; after he had

---

[21] Woodrup, now known as Woodrolfe

walked with Cobb a mile and a half on the sea wall he told him something serious had occurred, and he must prepare to meet it; Cobb said, "I suppose then my wife or child has been murdered?" this took place about a quarter of a mile from Cobb's home; Cobb had previously to this been questioned by the police as to where he had left his razor and pocket knife; I told Cobb his wife had been murdered.

Cross-examined. I am only here by accident, and have not been subpoenaed; I was one of the Coroner's Jury in this case.

Elizabeth Orrin, a tea-hawker, living at Colchester, deposed.--- On the morning of the murder I was at Tollesbury; I called at Cobb's house about 5 minutes past eight and lifted up the latch of the house twice, but could not get in, as it was locked; I was in the habit of calling at Cobb's house regularly once a fortnight about the same time, but never before found the door locked; I went to two or three other places and returned to Cobb's cottage about a quarter to nine; I again tried the door and rapped very loudly, upon which I heard a child cry out, "Oh!, my mother is dead," I gave an alarm, and the child having thrown the key out of the window, Mrs. Wash opened the door with it. I, Mrs. Wash and Mrs. Sampson, then went into the house and upstairs found the deceased with her throat cut.

Cross-examined by Mr. Parry It was a quarter to nine when I went the second time; I considered Mrs. Wash's clock too slow.

Johnathan Nicholls, coast-guard officer at Tollesbury, examined.

I heard the alarm of murder and went to the deceased house a little before nine o'clock; there were one or two in the house before me; the deceased was lying dead in bed on her left side with her left hand across her breast; there was no blood on either of her hands; there was no appearance of disorder about the bed-clothes; the wearing apparel, both in Cobb's and the lodger's room, was thrown about the floor; the crib in which the child slept was about two feet from the bed, and the deceased slept on the further side of the bed from the crib.

Cross-examined by Mr. Parry. Her hand was quite cold; there was a great quantity of blood in the bed; I observed a spot of blood on the floor, near the dresser, but I did not see any on the clothes or the box.

Samuel Home, harness-maker at Tollesbury, also got to the cottage about nine o'clock; he went to the head of the bed and put his hand underneath the deceased's head to see if there was any instrument underneath it, but put the hand in the same place again; there was a great deal of blood, and it was warm.

Cross-examined by Mr. Parry. Saw some blood on one of the hatchers belonging to one of the lodgers; I did not see any on the linen; the string of the deceased's night-cap was divided and one part of it saturated in blood.

Mr. Wm. Smyth, surgeon, of Tolleshunt D'Arcy, examined. I reached Cobb's house about 20 minutes of or half-past nine, I found her in bed, and she appeared to have been dead about two hours; the body was warm, but the upper extremities were cold; I found a large wound of about four inches in length, in the throat dividing the trachea; it was such an injury as might have been inflicted by a razor; I should say the wound was cut from left to right, and the party inflicting it would most probably have stood between the bed and the crib; I also found a fracture of the upper side of the temple bone, above the ear and a little in front; the skull was fractured into several pieces, and that must have been the consequence of a violent blow with some blunt instrument; a hammer would be a very likely instrument to produce such a wound; it is not probable that the wound was inflicted by the hedge stake which I have seen produced, but it is not impossible; there was also an incised wound on the upper lip --- probably about a quarter of an inch in depth; there were also two or three slight wounds on the scalp; the effect of the blow on the skull would be to deprive the party of sensibility.

Cross-examined by Mr. Parry. I saw the hedge stake and hammer produced at the inquest; when I first saw the body, I stated my opinion that the wound was not inflicted by a razor; that was my first impression.

Mr. Parry: Did you not after mature reflection adhere in that opinion?

Mr. Smyth: No; I stated the possibility of its having been inflicted by a razor.

Mr. Parry: Have you not insisted that you adhered to your first impression, although your mind must necessarily have been influenced in consequence of the razor having been found?

Mr. Smyth: No; I don't think I did adhere to my first opinion.

Mr. Parry: What then is the opinion you now desire to give?

Mr. Smyth: I cannot say what it was done with; I think it very possible it was done with a razor.

Mr. Parry: Is it not very probable that it was not done with a razor?

Mr. Smyth: My impression is now that it was inflicted by a razor; I have not discussed the matter with Mr. Dawson and with Professor Taylor; my opinion is that the wound was made from left to right; I could not say in the first instance whether it was made from right tom left or from left to right.

Mr. Parry: Have you not expressed your opinion that the party inflicting the wound would have his hand and arm soaked with blood?

Mr. Smyth: Most probably his hand would have blood upon it; the spurt of blood upwards would be more violent from one than two arteries; I should say certainly that the hand, unless the bed-clothes interfered, would be covered with blood and the same would also most probably be the case with the arm.

By his Lordship: I should not think the blow was inflicted by the hedge stake, as it did not correspond with the impression on the skull, which fitted exactly with the hammer.

Mr. John Dawson, surgeon, of Tolleshunt D'Arcy, examined.

I got to the house of Cobb about two o'clock in the afternoon; I immediately formed the opinion that the wound in the throat must have been inflicted by a razor or some sharp instrument; it was made from left to right; there were jags in the wound which would render it physically impossible that it could have been made from right to left; I have no doubt the blow would produce instantaneous unconsciousness; the blow would produce concuss, but that would not affect the flow of blood immediately and perhaps not at all; I believe that the woman was first knocked on the head before the injury to the throat; either injury would have caused death, but the blow on the skull might have been survived for some time; before the razor was found I made a sketch of the shape of the instrument which had caused the wound.

Cross-examined by Mr. Parry. It would depend upon the position of the party inflicting the wound whether or not the hand and arm would be covered with blood; if the party stood behind the deceased at the time he might have escaped the blood, but in all probability the hand would have blood upon it; but it would be less likely to have blood upon it if the wound were inflicted quickly; no doubt when the razor got into the wound the party used great force; as the edge of the razor was blunted by coming against the bone; the carotid artery on the right side was cut, but not on the left side.

Mr. Parry: Do you now agree with Mr. Smyth that the blood would flow much more violently if only one artery were cut?

Mr. Dawson: I think it makes little or no difference.

By his Lordship: By the wound being left to right I mean that the wound commenced at the left ear; from the direction of the wound I should say the murdered woman must have been lying on her left side, and her head must have been drawn back when the wound was inflicted.

By Mr. Parry: The bark on the window sill corresponded with that of the hedge stake; the hammer could not have produced the whole injury with a single blow; the stake might have done it, but it was too light an instrument to have caused such a fracture without very great violence. When I saw the hedge stake it was broken in the middle.

By Mr. Bodkin: There was not a single abrasion of the skin on the skull, but that might have been accounted for by the nightcap being on. I practice in the same village with Mr. Smyth.

By his Lordship: It was quite impossible that the unfortunate woman could have inflicted the wound herself.

James Coates, dredgerman. I lodged at Wash's house with my son and the prisoner on the night preceding the murder. I, my son and the prisoner got up between five and six; I had the need to go to the garden and on my return to Wash's house the prisoner went up towards the privy; about six o'clock I went to my work dredging and when I got to my boat I found Cobb, my son, and Wash there.

Cross-examined by Mr. Parry. The privy the prisoner was going to was communal to the four houses. I am not certain as to the time, but can speak to a quarter of an hour. No one keeps pigs in that yard; there is a pigsty, but it is uninhabited. (Laughter)

Mary Wash. I am sister of the prisoner and live in a cottage opposite to Mr. Cobb's. I remember about 9 o'clock in the morning of the murder hearing a little girl scream; I did not go in the house directly; Mrs. Orrin came and spoke to me; she went to the cottage and I afterwards went; I went into the cottage with Mrs. Orrin, and went upstairs and saw Mrs. Cobb lying on the left side covered with blood. I did not notice the boxes at first, but I went up into the room some time afterwards and found the contents of the boxes turned out; I do not know who went up between the time that I first went up and the second time; another of the neighbours --- Mrs. [ineligible] and others were there. I have known Cobb and his wife about two years. I believe they lived happily together. The prisoner lodged at my house and also a man named Coates, and his two sons and no other person besides myself and husband lived in the house; my husband got up just before six, and the other persons soon afterwards; Harrington went out just as my husband went out, and went up the garden; I heard him come in soon afterwards, and I called for a light, and my brother brought it to me. About three quarters of an hour afterwards I came downstairs, my brother had called to me to know if he should make a fire. He went out soon after; I judge it was about seven; it was getting quite light. He did not come to my house any more that day. I am quite sure he did not return before the child cried. I cannot say whether he had the same clothes on when apprehended as when he went out. I think about a quarter of an hour after my brother went I heard some person pass my door. I thought it was my neighbour, for it was quite a light step, and the sound seemed to be going towards the gate, which would lead to Salcot. I remember being applied to by the police for my brother's handkerchiefs; I did not give them any, but the policeman found two --- one, a blue one, by the side of the prisoner's bed, and another in his pocket, but the latter was my husband's, which I had lent him. I told the policeman my brother had a pink handkerchief, pale with washing. I was shown a handkerchief at the inquest. I did not see any blood upon it. On the Monday afterwards, I showed to Mr. Cook another pink handkerchief which I had found on the Saturday after the murder in my drawers. I am quite sure the one I found was my brother's; it was lighter in colour than the other; I had been to the drawer before I found this handkerchief, but had not turned the things. I did not know my brother was suspected until Mr. Cook told me so. My husband had the razor to shave with on Sunday, and I believe the prisoner also; It think I saw it on the window on Monday, but am not sure; there was no particular place for it; Fox came and asked me about the razor, but I did not then see it in the window, and both Fox and my husband looked for it.

Cross-examined by Mr. Parry. My house was full of persons soon after the murder was discovered; there are persons living close to us; it was quite in the evening time of Wednesday that I then heard my brother was in custody for the murder; I am not sure I was examined before the Jury before I knew that my brother was in custody; I was examined very fully before the Coroner; I heard my brother about six he had lighted the fire; he was getting his breakfast ready; I do not know the time of my brother going out, except that it was getting light; I believe it was nearly seven. I do not whether it was Mr. Cook or Mr. Archer to whom I gave the handkerchief I found; I do not know whether the handkerchief was kept back from the Coroner for some days. I think it was almost three-quarters of an hour after my clock struck six that I heard him finally go out; my clock was half an hour slower than the real time. I know the hammer which was taken from the house; it was taken from the coal place by Mr. Fox or Mr. Cook; If my brother had taken the hammer out of the coal place he could not have put it back without my knowing it; he must come into the house and open the closet door to do it; I was in the house from the time my brother went out until about ten o'clock. A short time before the time of the murder, perhaps a month or five weeks, my brother had killed a pig; I also remember my brother bringing in another pig pluck in a handkerchief about a month before the murder --- they were dripping in blood. I remember having seen my brother put ink upon the edge of his hat when it was getting worn. I know my husband was in the habit of using the razor. Mrs. Cobb was at my house the day before the murder, and very merry with us; my brother knew we were on very friendly terms with the Cobbs, and he was so also; I knew before the murder my brother was going to Wivenhoe for a boat, and when he went out I thought he was going about the boat.

John Wash examined. On the morning of the murder I left home about eight minutes before six o'clock. Coates's boy went out with me, and Coates came shortly afterwards. Cobb came down about five minutes afterwards.

Mr. Solly being recalled, proved that the church clock was very irregularly kept.

Joseph Kiev, waterman, of Tollesbury, examined. On the morning in question I got up about half past six o'clock, in going to my work towards Salcot I observed a man at the end of Cobb's cottage, about ten minutes to seven; he was standing against the school yard gate; it was not light; when he got against Wash's gate he went into the yard; I could not distinguish the features of the party; I have known the prisoner from a boy; I noticed the height and general form of the man, and I believe it to have been the prisoner; I don't know whether he had anything on his head, but if he had it was a cap.

Cross-examined by Mr. Parry. I would not undertake to swear that it was the prisoner; it was not quite light enough; my evidence was taken for the first time on Tuesday, at Mr. Parker's; I knew the inquest was adjourned, but did not go forward with my evidence because I was not called for; Mr. Fox, the policeman, came to me about my evidence, but I can't say how long since; I mentioned the circumstances to Coates soon after the prisoner had his hearing.

Mr. Parry: Did not the prisoner's father come to you and ask whether you knew anything about the matter, and did you not say the report was false?

Witness: I told him not to make himself uneasy about it; I never saw any one jump over the hedge.

Re-examined. The father met me at the Plough on the [illegible] and said there was a report that I had seen some one jump over the hedge, and that if I did it must be his unfortunate son; upon which I told him not to make himself uneasy, for I had seen no one jump over the hedge; I have never had any quarrel with the prisoner or his family.

Elijah Bowles, fish-hawker. of Tollesbury, examined. About a quarter past seven on the morning of the murder, I saw the prisoner coming from the gate that leads to the yard common to Cobb's and Wash's houses. I was about 30 yards from him, and we met one another; he was going towards Salcot; he had on light fustian trousers; I don't recollect the coat he had on; he wore a cap.

Cross-examined by Mr. Parry. I know the prisoner well; I asked him if he had any winkles to sell, and he said "no, he was going turnipping" He was walking middling quick did not observe anything agitated about his manner; he was coming out of the gate common to his own house and well as that of Cobb.

Re-examined. It was light enough to distinguish a person at about 20 yards.

Abraham Foukes, porter, of Salcot, examined. On the morning of the murder I saw the prisoner in the footpath between Tollesbury and Salcot; there is a woolve or culvert in the path over which the prisoner had to pass; it is about two and a half miles from where I saw the prisoner to the edge of Tollesbury. I was scraping my shoes at my own door when the prisoner overtook me, and I said, "good morning, Henry", but he made me no answer, nor took any notice of me; the prisoner was only about a yard from me, when I saw him at first, he was only about 30 rods from me.

Cross-examined by Mr. Parry. The prisoner had to cross a stile and when I saw him he was about twenty rods from it; I had not been out all night; I had no quarrel with the prisoner about any vegetables, nor with his father.

Mr. Parry: Have you ever been in any little trouble or difficulty?

Witness: Do I paid for it. (Laughter)

Mr. Parry: Very handsome of you I am sure. But have you never been imprisoned?

Witness: I since paid £1 for killing a hare, and another time I got three months for the same thing. (Laughter)

John Foakes, labourer, of Salcot, deposed. On Wednesday the 26th, the day after the murder, I was watching a coursing party between three and four o'clock, near the stile in the footpath to Salcot; I looked down into the ditch, and saw an impression of a shoe upon the grass, and underneath the woolve. I picked up the pocket handkerchief and razor and case now produced; both the handkerchief and razor had bloodstains upon them; I handed them to Mr. Dawson, surgeon.

Cross-examined by Mr. Parry. The party putting the razor and handkerchief under the woolve must have stooped down to do so; a great many labourer and others frequent the path in question at an early hour of the morning in going to their work.

Abraham Emery, labourer, of Salcot, examined --- I am the prisoner's cousin; on the morning of the murder he met me at Salcot, and there we bought a boat of Mr. Barton, for which I paid £1 down and we were to pay the rest weekly; the boat was not ready when we went to Wivenhoe, and we did not pay the money over for it. I asked the prisoner a week before how much money he could get, and he replied about 10s.; on the day before the murder I was at Tollesbury, and asked the prisoner how much money he had, upon which, he showed me 8s. 6d. As we went to Wivenhoe the prisoner showed me a letter which he said he had to leave at the Lion Inn, Abberton; he subsequently put a stamp on the letter and posted it at Fingrington[22]. We then went to Wivenhoe, and saw Mr. Barton, but did not pay him anything on account of the boat; we had some beer at Wivenhoe, and returned to Salcot, where we had supper at Young's beer-house. On our return we heard of the terrible affair at Tollesbury. The same night policeman Fox came to the Rising Sun, and took the prisoner aside for some conversation.

Cross-examined by Mr. Parry. There was an agreement with three of us to purchase the boat in question, but the third party go out of it; the prisoner met me by appointment at a quarter past eight o'clock on the morning of the murder, there was nothing extraordinary about the prisoner's conduct; he had a letter to post to a party at Mersea. As we were coming home the prisoner slipped down on the river wall, and slipped down on his back for a yard or more; it was a muddy place, but I did not take any notice as to whether his trousers were dirty from it; I slept with the prisoner that night at Salcot, and was with him until he was taken to the inquest on the following day. The murder was talked of in the tap room of the Rising Sun, and it was spoken as an extraordinary thing that the child should have slept so near the bed on which the mother was murdered; the prisoner went with Beckwith, the policeman, to Tollesbury, very quietly, and without handcuffs; the prisoner's father told me that his mother had

---

[22] **No longer exists**

given the prisoner some money on the night before the murder; he did not tell me that his mother was going to borrow 10s. for him.

Re-examined by Mr. Bodkin. I had finished my breakfast when the prisoner came to me at Salcot to go to Wivenhoe.

John Foakes, being recalled by Mr. Parry, proved that the night before the murder the prisoner's mother borrowed of him 10s amongst which there were two half-crowns; witness was aware the prisoner's father and mother came to the inquest for the purpose of giving evidence.

Mr. W Codd, Coroner, pressed that at the inquest he asked the prisoner if he wished to be examined as a witness, prisoner replied "As you please, Sir." He (Mr. Codd) told him since it was not as he pleased, but as the prisoner pleased, for he was now in custody on suspicion, and he (Mr. Codd) did not think it right to examine him, he then asked him if he had any objection to be examined; he replied that he had not, he (Mr. Codd) then told him he was required to answer any questions which might lead to incriminate himself, indeed he added that he should not require him to answer any questions unless he wished to do so; he then asked the prisoner if he had understood his position, and he replied that he did; his deposition was then taken and read over to him.

(The deposition here read, and which we published at the time, was, for the most part a confirmation of Emery's evidence, the prisoner stated in it that he left home for Salcot on the morning of the murder with three-shilling pieces only in his pocket, and also that he possessed only one pocket handkerchief).

In cross-examination, Mr. Codd said the prisoner answered all the questions put to him without the least hesitation, and in the most straightforward manner. The handkerchief was not produced at the adjourned inquest until after Mr. Codd called for it. He did not go on to ask the prisoner whether his mother had given him any money when he reached Salcot.

James Jenkins, beer-shop keeper, at Wivenhoe, proved that the prisoner came to his house alone on the morning of the 25th November between 11 and 12 o'clock, and paid for a pint of beer with a half-crown.

Cross-examined, I had never seen the prisoner before and did not see him again till the inquest, when he was in custody.

Mary Ann Wenlock, servant at the Ship at Launch, Wivenhoe, said that Jenkins's beer-house was only a few steps from her house; on the 25th of Nov. the prisoner came in the tap room of the former house, and she took from the prisoner a half-crown in payment for two pints of beer.

Cross-examined. Mr. Barton said the witness Emery came in the tap room and they all appeared to be drinking together.

William Elijah Wallford, shoemaker, of Wivenhoe, examined. I was at the Ship at Launch, Wivenhoe, on the afternoon of the 25th of Nov., last, and saw the prisoner there; his father and Emery were with him between two and three o'clock, and shortly after that he was alone with me, when he drew up close by me and told me he did not like working on the land for 16d a day.

Charles Last, miller, of Salcot. On the 25th of November, last, I was at the Rising Sun, Salcot, between nine and ten at night, in company with the prisoner, Emery and a "room full"; I heard the prisoner say, "It appears to me almost impossible for anyone to go up and murder the woman without waking the child, for it only lay two feet from the mother's bed; before this I heard nothing mentioned about the child.

Cross-examined by Mr. Parry. A man in the room said he heard it was only a step from the bed, and the prisoner said it might be thereabouts; I had heard the murder spoken of before that; I went in rather late; I did not hear anyone else express surprise about the matter besides the prisoner.

Policeman Fox, examined. I was called in, in consequence of the discovery of the murder of the deceased; I went over to Salcot for the prisoner the same morning, but did not find him there; I went again about ten o'clock the same night, and got him to strip himself; I found 1s. 5 ½ d. upon him; there was no blood on his shirt, the sleeves of which were short; I noticed mud on both sides and thighs of the prisoner's trousers, and asked him how he came all over mud; he said he had slipped from the sea wall; I told him it was very odd that both the back and front part of the trousers should be dirtied that way; he said, "I suppose you are examining me on account of the Tollesbury murder;" but I gave him no reply; I told the prisoner he must be at the King's Head at Tollesbury either at ten or eleven the next morning; he replied that Emery and he were coming to Tollesbury the next morning and he would undertake to be there at the time; on the following morning he was brought to Tollesbury by Beckwith, the constable; I then noticed that where I had the night previous [ineligible] there were black spots, and the trousers appeared to have been [ineligible]; I also observed some red spots both above and below the black ones; I pointed them out and the prisoner said, "I know nothing about them." I afterwards saw the prisoner standing at Beckwith's door, when he said, "I carried a pig's pluck the other day, and blood might have come upon my trousers from that;" on the day of the murder I found the hedge stake produced here today in the ozier ground near Cobb's cottage; I also found a piece of bark on the window sill of the lower room in the cottage, and the coal-houses of Wash's cottage I found the hammer produced.

William Beckwith, parish constable, apprehended the prisoner at the Rising Sun, Salcot, on the morning after the murder; he told him he wanted him to go to Tollesbury with him, and he went willingly; witness showed some black spots and some red spots below them; nothing passed with respect to them, and the prisoner said nothing about the murder.

Cross-examined. The prisoner said, in answer to my observations. "I am ready to go when you are."

Superintendent Cook stated that on pointing out to the prisoner some blood on his trousers, he said, "I took some pig's pluck home. But I am innocent of that I know;" the trousers were forwarded to Professor Taylor.

Policeman Archer afterwards had the prisoner in custody, and on laying the trousers on the table produced said, "I don't know how the blood spots came unless they are from the killing;"

The case was adjourned at seven o'clock on Thursday night until the morning Friday, at nine o'clock, when the examination of witnesses was resumed.

The second day is taken from the *Essex Herald* full report of the trial, 9th March 1852.

Friday

The trial resumed this morning at nine o'clock.

John Clarke, examined by Mr. Bodkin. I am one of the officers of the gaol, and have measured the prisoner; he is 5 feet 7 ½ inches high.

James Pudney, examined by Mr. Bodkin. I am a labourer, living in Wigborough, four or five miles from Tollesbury. About a fortnight before the murder, I saw the prisoner at Colchester, and we walked home together, when he asked me if I had any money; I told him I had none; he said, "Nor have I; I want some, and some I must have;" I asked him where he meant to get it, whether he intended to steal it. He said, "No, but I know where there is some, and I don't sleep far from it when I am at home, and I mean to have it."

Cross-examined by Mr. Parry. I heard of the inquest, but I did not go; I heard of the murder, but I can't say if it was one or two days after it; I heard on the third day after the murder that Harrington was suspected; about a week after I heard of the murder, I mentioned this conversation to Mr. Fox; I went to Mr. Parker's office on Tuesday last for the first time, when my evidence was first taken. I have never been in prison, nor have I been in trouble; I may be, I can't tell what may happen. I was with the prisoner at Colchester on the latter part of the day.

Re-examined. I saw Fox at Great Wigborough a week after the murder, and told him about it; I received instructions on Saturday last to go to Mr. Parker's; I came to Chelmsford on Tuesday last; I have not received a farthing for coming.

By Mr. Parry. I left home early on the Monday, slept at Boreham Lion, and arrived at nine or half past or ten o'clock; I spent some money on my way. I went into one beer house on my journey. There were six of us coming. I paid my own expenses. I believe I do expect to get some. I expected that before I left Wigborough. I have been staying at Chelmsford since last Tuesday, and trust to the liberality of the conductors of this prosecution. I don't think it is a capital job.

Mr. Parry: Don't you?

Witness: No

Mr. Parry. Why, you've been laughing during the whole of your examination. It appears you think very lightly of such an affair as this.

Re-examined by Mr. Bodkin. I had 2. 6d. in my pocket when I started.

Fox, p.c. recalled by Mr. Bodkin. I went and saw the last witness ten days after the murder, when he made a communication to me; that was after the adjournment inquest. I went to Wigborough last Saturday to see the witnesses who were to come to Mr. Parker's on Tuesday last.

Thomas Rawlinson examined by Mr. Rodwell. I am bailiff to Mr. Fairhead of Tollesbury Hall, and know the prisoner; on the Saturday previous to the murder I paid the prisoner 1s., and he came to his work on the Monday; it was frosty, and he earned but little, as he was paid by the acre; he had not finished his job on the Monday; he had earned only that 2s. the week before --- I do not know of his working that week for anybody else.

Cross-examined. He was pulling turnips, and for some days in the frost he could not pull; that is all he earned with me, and that is all I gave him.

Hezekiah Catchmead, examined by Mr. Bodkin. I am a dredgerman at Tollesbury, and live in the building adjoining Wash's house --- it is one house, but three hirings; the persons who lived there at the time of the murder were A Bolton, who lodged with me, three of the Leapers and Robert Constable in another tenement, and Wash was the third. On Monday I was out to have my boat repaired, went home and went to bed, got up at half past twelve, took my boat and was away till between two and three on the Tuesday afternoon; Bolton was with me all the time, and we returned together.

Argent Bolton examined by Mr. Bodkin. I lodge with the last witness, and was with him as stated, till we returned between two and three o ['clock on the Tuesday.

James Leaper, a labourer. On the morning of the murder I went to my work at Mr. Solly's. at a quarter before five, and returned about three; my father is nearly blind and very aged; he was home in bed when I left.

William Leaper, examined by Mr. Bodkin. I live with the last witness. I had nothing to do that morning, and did not get up till eight o'clock; when I heard of the murder at nine o'clock, I went out of the house; I had not been so before that morning.

John Leaper, the father, an old man. I got up at eight, and had not been out of the cottage that morning, till I heard of the murder.

Robert Constable, labourer. On the morning of the murder I was in an ill state of health, and did not go out of the house till I heard of the murder.

Rice.: I live at Tollesbury, and attend to the parish clock; at that time the clock by the real time was 20 minutes too fast --- I set it so myself; I have now put it back 20 minutes, and find it is the right time; I found the right time by the railway.

Cross-examined. I have managed the clock 8 years; I knew it was too fast.

John Wash was recalled by Mr. Bodkin., and the razor put into his hand. I am sure I cannot swear this was my razor --- mine was black. (Examined it, and opened it). My razor was as near as could be straight in the back.

Mr. Bodkin: Is it like your razor?

Witness: The handle is, but I thought the blade was not like it.

Mr. Bodkin: Was your razor like that?

Witness. The handle was.

Cross-examined. I thought it was not my razor by the blade. The razor I had I bought in the State of Maine, in America, 11 or 12 years ago; It had on the blade --- "who buys me, will not repent;" I think it was not cut, but put on in some way; but there was the inscription plain enough when I bought it; if a person opens the coal house at my house, it covers the space of the cottage door; on going into the cottage the hinges are on the right; The cottage door opens on the inside, and has a latch that lifts rather heavy; to get at the coal house a person would be forced to open the front door and throw it back, and the coal house door, when opened, would fill the space of the cottage door within four to five inches.

Re-examined. I last used my razor on Sunday; and either laid it on the window sill or in the little drawer; --- I think I saw it on the Monday; I never saw it after; I have looked everywhere.

By the Court. I do not remember the name on the case; I do not know there was a name on it; I bought it at the same the same time as the razor; the razor had been ground several times, to the best of my recollection the case had red inside at the top.

The Judge: Then do you not believe this is your razor?

Witness: I really can't say; the handle and case are like, but I thought the blade was different.

The Judge: What is your belief on the subject? You are on your oath you know.

Witness: I thought the blade of the razor was hardly heavy enough for mine which I missed, which was an extraordinary large razor.

The Judge: Then you don't believe this is yours?

Witness: I thought it was not large enough in the blade, and I told Mr. Codd so.

The Judge: Have you always been of that opinion?

The Witness: That was the reason I could not swear to it at the coroner's inquest.

The Judge: Have you always been of that opinion, and always so expressed yourself?

The Witness: Yes: I could not swear to it.

The Judge: How long is it since you saw the inscription on your razor?

The Witness: Not for eight or nine years.

James Digby, examined by Mr. Bodkin. I some time since lodged at Cobb's house; about a twelve months ago, Cobb said to shave me; I don't know anything about the razor now produced; It was like it, but I did not notice it sufficiently to state my belief.

Coates recalled by Mr. Bodkin. I have shaved with the razor used by Cobb, the property of Wash. The razor case is like the one of Wash's, having a broken place in it; I never noticed any particularity about the razor.

James Cobb, recalled by Mr. Bodkin. I have been in the habit of using Wash's razor nearly two years; I have shaved myself and other... [illegible section] ...

Cross-examined by Mr. Parry. The back window was fastened in the morning; I never knew it opened unless someone opened it. It was fastened overnight.

Mr. P. Chancellor, the surveyor of the plans, in answer to Mr. Bodkin, said --- as one enters Wash's door it turns to the left; it opens inwards, and the coal house is on the right hand. The coal door is two feet nine inches; supposing the coal door to be opened and the front door opened, the coal door would be covered about a foot.

Professor Taylor, of Guy's Hospital, examined by Mr. Bodkin. I have examined some articles delivered to me by the police; and in the first place I examined a pair of fustian trousers, which are now produced. I observed the front of the right leg some spots of a reddish colour, something like blood; others of a blacker hue, like ink stains, had blood under them. I examined them with a very powerful microscope, of 40,000 power. The result of my examination was undoubtedly the red stains were from blood; with regard to one, not quite covered with the ink, I observed a small distinct clot of blood in the fibre of the material. I am not positive that under all the ink spots blood was found, because some were completely discoloured that I could not tell; these appear to have been rubbed; the ink was very thick upon them; higher up the trousers I found red spots not covered; there were three very slight ones, having been rubbed --- they are blood; one was near to the right hand pocket; there was another spot at the back of the right thigh on a level with the spots in front; two were found, one a very minute one, apparently not rubbed at all; they were both blood, having a clot in it; the spots covered with the ink appear to be larger and more conspicuous in front of the thigh. As to the jacket handed to me by Cooke, the one worn by the prisoner, I examined the right hand pocket and found upon the lining a smear of blood; I have also examined the trousers found at the house, and upon the lining of the right hand pocket I found a large and very distinct stain of blood; I found nothing very particular about the trousers; they were very dirty, and I found no ink; they are very much worn, nearly worn up; the old jacket I examined and found a distinct stain of blood upon the right hand pocket; there was no appearance of rubbing upon them or the last mentioned trousers. We cannot distinguish between the blood of human being and that of a pig; there is a small distinction, but not sufficient to place reliance upon.

By the Court. I could not tell how long the blood had been there; it might have been there 2, 6 or 8 months. The things were brought to me on the 11th February.

By Mr. Bodkin. After four or five days or a week, we cannot make a distinction when it was first put on; I found upon the blade a thick stain of blood on both sides, [illegible] the back of the razor, such as would be produced by a cut attended with much bleeding; the short portion of the razor was wiped as it were by drawing through a wound. I applied a microscope and chemical tests to a portion of the stain, and found it composed of a portion of blood and iron rust. About the middle of the edge of the razor where there was a small clot of blood, I found two or three very minute fibres which turned out to be cotton. I saw no letters but those of the maker's name upon the blade, but it had evidently been ground and that more than once; there was blood upon both sides of the handle, inside, as if from the blade being shut while wet with blood; there was no blood on the outside of the handle. The inscription would in all probability have been removed by grinding. I think it a large sized razor.

Mr. Parry objected to Dr. Taylor stating that the razor was a large one.

His Lordship would strike that out then.

Dr. Taylor. I have seen a good many razors, and I should describe it as a large one; I heard the material evidence yesterday as to; in my judgement I believe it might have been inflicted by the razor we are speaking of. The injury to the head would be likely to stagnate the circulation of the blood; the effect of one of the carotid arteries being cut would not, I think, affect the flow of blood; looking to the state of the razor, and assuming that was the instrument, the wound might have been made with great rapidity, especially if the person was insensible; I should not infer from the state of the razor that the wound was hastily made. Supposing the wound made from left to right, and the person inflicting such a wound standing behind, the man might escape all blood, but it would depend upon the rapidity with which the wound was made; such as one might be made in from five to ten seconds, where there was no resistance; before the external carotid artery was divided the hand would be away from the head; of the string of the woman's cap was cut, and that made of cotton, it might account for the cotton found in the film of blood on the razor.

By his Lordship: There is no confounding woollen with cotton fibre?

By. Mr. Bodkin. I think the blow on the head must have been inflicted with great violence and I think by the hammer; I think the stake was not a likely instrument to inflict such a blow; and if it did the injury would be less from the breaking of it. I [illegible]

With the exception of one being more [illegible] they were alike. Taking the whole of the injuries, they might have been inflicted in two or three minutes. A blow which produced the appearance found, would produce immediate insensibility.

Cross-examined. I should have been better able to judge had I personally examined the head, but I think the description given sufficiently clear. Although I should prefer a personal examination which would be safer for me to act upon. My impression is that the person might escape blood; The blood would more likely spurt towards the head of the bed, at right angles, thrown out by jerks. Supposing the murderer standing behind the blood would have gone from the hand, but if immediately followed, the heart would have less effect upon the blood, although it would have come out at right angles to the instrument. After a week it is not able to form a safe opinion as to when the blood was put on – I could not at all in this case. Certainly; after ten days a clot of blood, I know, would not alter its appearance for five years. I have submitted the fustian trousers to microscope test; I consider the microscope an infallible test, after having examined spots of blood for many years. Ink is composed of sulphate of iron, but that cannot be mistaken for blood; nor when used alone would it be confounded for blood; sulphate of iron is green; my opinion is not formed upon the colour of three spots, but upon the coagulum of blood. Sulphate of Iron would become oxidised if it had time.

By Mr. Bodkin. If I find congulum of a red colour, I am certain it is blood; I have no doubt about these spots being blood. I am quite unable to give an opinion as to how the blood came upon these trousers.

By the Court. Any blunt instrument, or a round stone, with great force would have inflicted the wound.

Cobb, recalled by Mr. Bodkin. The night cap of my wife was made of white cotton.

By Mr. Parry. I don't know that a hedge stake was cut out of my hedge.

Fox recalled by Mr. Parry. I found the stake in two hanging together. I examined the hedge of Cobb's and found a stake had been freshly taken out, near the school-yard gate.

Mrs. Wash recalled by his Lordship. I saw one drop of blood upon Mason's box; it looked quite fresh; I also saw one upon the floor at the foot of the bed, and one upon the stairs. As far as I know this razor is different to the one of my husband's. The blade does not look so thick, neither does the handle. The case was black like this.

This being the case for the prosecution.

Mr. Parry then addressed the jury for the prisoner.

I have now, he said, to attempt to discharge a duty cast on me under circumstances which I, knowing what I do of the profession to which I belong, believing as I do that in an emergency of this kind, an advocate, however feeble his power may be, may render some service to the interests of justice and truth, have been compelled by this feeling to undertake; but I assure you, without the slightest affectation, that I feel most deeply oppressed in the performance of that duty, not I hope to an extent that will disable me from completing that which I have gone through hitherto, but I feel deeply oppressed in the situation in which I am placed, for there is a living human being in this court who awaits a verdict at your hands that may consign him to death, and annihilate his existence; and upon me, to some extent, to a great extent, devolves this fearful responsibility. It is my duty to do everything that I fairly and honourably can do, in order to avert that, and I feel oppressed by this strong sense within me, that I may by possibility, not to do that duty as it ought to be done. I cannot consider anything more awful that this situation in which you, my Lord, and I stand at this time. We have heard all the witnesses examined at great length, the evidence has been patiently and carefully taken; and I have now to address you on that evidence --- I have to suggest to you those topics which I think fairly may be urged on behalf of the wretched lad at the bar; and you afterwards will have to decide on his fate --- you twelve gentlemen, by the merest accident, brought into that box --- you are to say shall this young man live or cease to live. I do not believe in all the range of human institutions there is anything of so fearful, so tremendous a power as that you are called on to exercise; feeling this so strongly as I do, I am only sustained by a firm and abiding conviction that you will not consign that young man to the scaffold unless you are satisfied of his guilt almost as thoroughly as if you with your own eyes had seen the murder committed. He (Mr. P) believed upon cases of this kind advocates of a far greater experience than he had endeavoured to cast the crime back upon other individuals, and by so doing they had seriously damaged themselves and their clients. He was not going to do so --- he was not there to say upon whom the guilt was; but they were here to say whether the young man at the bar was guilty or innocent, and under no circumstances could they be asked the question --- who else is the guilty party? Unless they felt, by the force of the evidence, that this young man was guilty, --- unless they felt that, they could not pronounce an adverse verdict. They had not to inquire who else could have done it, or whether there were any other guilty parties. Had they seen anything which enabled them to fix it upon any other individuals; --- that was not the question which could be submitted to them. It was the bounden duty of the prosecution to bring home the guilt of the accused. The law of England probably differed in that respect from the criminal law of almost every other nation, except, perhaps, the United States, which was kindred with this country. In other countries it was for the criminal to show himself innocent. In England fortunately for those who live here, it was left for the crown to show who was guilty. If that duty were sacred and incumbent in one case more than in another, it was in the case of life or death. He did say it was the duty of the prosecution to prove the case, and especially where they were called upon to say whether the prisoner should live or die. He earnestly trusted that he might be able to demonstrate to them (although he would make no pledges, that the prisoner was innocent of the charge). He would submit to them from the mode in which this prosecution was conducted from beginning to end, from the matter of the prosecution, that they had not brought home the guilt of the accused; far from that, they had almost demonstrated that it was impossible for him to have been the man. Suspicion of course had been aroused against this young man, but suspicion however strong, would not do; it must be a strong firm conviction, grasping, as it were, their minds, --- seizing upon the almost irresistibly, --- it was that, and that alone, upon which they could act. He said again, from the substance of the matter laid before them by the prosecution, there was not merely ample room to doubt, whether this young man could be guilty, but if some portion of the evidence for the pros were true, it appeared to him that the prisoner could hardly be supposed to be the murderer; let them look at the evidence; and let them remember the circumstantial evidence only became of value when all the circumstances of the case clung together in a most precise form.

Was there any anger, vindictiveness, or revenge suggested to them as operating upon the mind of the prisoner? There was none. Plunder had been suggested; that was probable, but it did not exclude the supposition that the woman might have been murdered by someone who had some other motive besides. He should examine, first, the manner and mode of this murder; next the conduct of the young man with reference to every fact and circumstance alleged, against him, and finally, say what were the general bearings and probabilities of the case. On Cobb, he did not hesitate to say, from the course of this case had taken, that if he (Mr. P.) attempted to make any insinuations against him he should be a disgrace to the profession he belonged to. Nothing had occurred in this case requiring it; if there had, he should not have shrunk from the duty, however open to misinterpretation.

But there was none, and God forbid he should make it. The questions put to him were not to show he was the murderer, but to show that a man might make use of expressions which really might be prejudicial to him, and create suspicion, though in reality there might be no ground for it; he asked Cobb, before you know your wife was murdered, did you ask, is my wife murdered? And he said he did --- an answer which had been cleared up by evidence of Mr. Solly. He said, just let them reflect on that, and see on what accident sometimes depended, for Mr. Solly as here from curiosity, and had been called, but if he had not been, what a deep mystery would have hung about this answer of Cobb. Then he said he told his wife he would go home at half-past one, and did not go till three. These were two circumstances that if not cleared up might have been of great importance. Now the manner of the murder he thought was important. Let them take it that it might have been done in a few minutes ---- that cottage was situated where there were swarms of similar cottages, occupied by dredgers and labourers, and persons in that class of society. It appeared perfectly clear, that the whole of Tollesbury knew Cobb had been about to purchase a boat; the cottage was situated on the high road to the river, where hundreds of fishermen passed daily, morning and evening, going to and coming from their work; when Cobb left the house the door was left on the latch, the poor woman and child quietly and innocently sleeping; any one might enter there, and he who did enter would take the dark of the morning to do it, when he was little likely to be observed. Therefore, time was of vast importance. The house was so situated, so exposed, known all over the whole neighbourhood to contain money, for it was the common talk of Tollesbury, on the high road, leading in the direction of the river at the entry of a village, with house after house crowded with inhabitants of the same class, and any one might have entered. His learned friend had virtually pledged himself to show them that the murder was committed with a razor and a hammer, a particular razor and a particular hammer, and he begged attention, to that --- not merely that a razor and hammer might have done it --- but he said in terms, I will demonstrate, to your satisfaction, as plainly as though you saw it done. I will bring it before your mind's eye as clearly, that it shall have the same effect as if you had with your physical eye seen it, that the razor of Wash, and the hammer from the coal house, are the things with which he did the deed. He could not say, I will show you a murder has been done, I will lay the facts before you and leave you to grope your way to a verdict of guilty. And here he must [illegible]…

…an extraordinary omission in his friend's opening. There was a plan produced, on which was marked the ozier bed lying on the border of the road, by which the dredgermen went every morning of their lives; a stake was found there and was in the hands of the police; his learned friend knew it as well as the policeman who found it, but not a syllable did he say about that stake in opening the case. Was not that an extraordinary omission; what, could he not reconcile the finding of that stake with the guilt of the prisoner? His learned friend had the painful duty cast on him of bringing home guilt to the prisoner, and the fact of the finding of this stake was wholly irreconcilable with his guilt. He believed his learned friend was afraid to mention it, for he knew he could not in any way account for it. If they in their own homes, in one apartment, were discussing how this murder was committed, who did it, and what were the facts connected with it, could they have omitted the circumstances of the stake. They would as soon have thought of leaving out the murder itself as the mention of this stake. How was this murder done? Was there any one of them who would take on himself to swear that the stake was not the instrument with which the murder was committed? If they should be of opinion that there was no doubt on that point, then it was entirely inconsistent with this young man's guilt, and with the theory set up by the prosecution.

What was the medical evidence about it? His friend did not altogether approve of Mr. Smith's evidence, and wanted to examine them as to whether they were not rival village doctors. Mr. Smith did not certainly give his evidence in a very clear manner --- he was a little nervous. Mr. Dawson was clearer --- and what did he say? That the hammer could only have produced death by repeated blows, but such a stake at one violent blow might have caused the fracture on the head of that unhappy woman. "Might have done it," was all that was necessary to say for the prisoner now before them. Dr. Taylor said he thought the hedge stake could not have inflicted the blow, but he said, "unless very great violence was used with it." This stake was freshly taken from the hedge of Cobb's garden --- there could be no mistake about it; and he believed in all human probability this was the instrument with which the murder was committed. It was found 20 yards off. On the sill of the window was found a little piece of bark corresponding with the bark on this stake. This was entirely inconsistent with the prisoner's guilt, because the ozier ground was in a different direction to that in which the prisoner went. Let them reflect on that. Then there was the hammer. Each of them looked at it, and when a man took a hammer in his hand, and heard that a murder had been committed with it, a sort of horror passed over him, and his judgement was for a moment unhinged. But let them look to the fact. His learned friend said, it was this hammer that did it. How did he show that? It was only an inference drawn from the most slender materials ever presented to his notice. They asked them to torture their minds into the belief that the prisoner used the hammer and took it back to the cottage, but Mrs. Wash was in it, and she never saw him. It was utterly impossible for that murder to have been committed with another hammer ---it might have been committed with some poker for aught he knew; but it was mathematically and logically demonstrated, that it was not committed with the hammer at Wash's. Next, then, was the razor. Was it Wash's razor? There was no proof this it was the razor belonging to Mr Wash --- it was only surmised that it was. Mr. and Mrs. Wash could not swear to it, although the maker's name was upon it, and that was a curious circumstance in this case, which he solemnly did believe to be a most mysterious one. Wash would not either today or at the inquest swear to the razor, and this is the razor with which the prosecution alleges the deed was committed, and these were the witnesses produced by the prosecution. The fact of Wash's razor being lost could not be pressed against him. Was the razor the one belonging to Wash? That was the question for them. He now came to an important, but not the all-important subject --- the prisoner's conduct in reference to this murder, how he spent the whole of his time, from the time he got up till he was taken into custody. There was a witness started on them this morning; who was never before the Coroner --- Pudney, who said, on the Saturday before the murder he had some conversation with the prisoner. This witness he had never heard of before, and he did not think it was wise and fair to keep back such a witness till the last. As to the witness himself, was he not making s holiday of it? Had he not the demeanour of a sharp clever fellow who came here recklessly and wantonly, and knowing the prisoner was waiting the sentence of death, yet in an almost grinning, almost revolting manner, he gave his evidence? Was there nothing for such a man in coming here to the court to receive payment of much greater amount that he could earn by his labour, and did not they think he had conducted himself in a manner that would make them receive his evidence with great caution. If the conversation did take place, what did it amount to? The conversation even if correctly reported, by a reckless and wanton witness, not as standing in the solemn presence of justice, but come for a lark to Chelmsford to hang someone, amounted to nothing. He asked the prisoner if he meant to steal the money, and he said, "No," but he said he knew where there was some money not far from where he slept, and he intended to have it; and they had it in evidence that this young man had got money from his mother. He might have some idea of borrowing money --- this man might have added words to the conversation, and was the life of a fellow creature to hang on a thread like that. The words might be tortured into a hundred meanings, but to infer from them that he meant to murder Mrs. Cobb was a result so awful that he shrunk from its contemplation. As to the course of the prisoner, it was not proved before them that he was anywhere where he ought not to have been --- or that he did anything that he ought not to have done --- or that he did anything out of his ordinary course of that day. Rice said he could not see the prisoner in the road because it was dark, but when he left his sister's house, she said it was daylight, and if the witness Rice could not swear to the prisoner, could they swear to him. As to the prisoner being seen in the school yard, he thought they would come to the conclusion that it was not proved to be the prisoner at the bar. This was another strong element of doubt. If that man was not the prisoner, and was the murderer, it might account for much that seemed to require explanation. Time was an important matter in this case. The prisoner's sister said that the prisoner got up at six o'clock, and remained in the house till three quarters of a hour after, and she thought it must be well to seven --- she meant by her clock, not by the time of day. It was daylight, which was important, because at ten minutes to seven it was not daylight; she said she came down, put her candles out, and dressed her child, and if anyone had entered she must have seen him. Just let them think of that in reference to Rice's evidence, which referred to ten minutes to seven, and if Mrs. Wash's evidence was true it could not be the prisoner, for he was not out in the dark. If Mrs. Wash's clock was half an hour too slow the prisoner left the house at a quarter past seven; if it was only ten minutes too slow he must have gone out five minutes before seven; the difference could not be beyond five or ten minutes one way or the other, and he pointed out this to call attention to the terrible difficulty there was to unravelling this mystery --- difficulties that might well appal them. His learned friend said the prisoner must have been at the school yard at ten minutes before seven. There was a serious mistake somewhere, and could they reconcile it. Did not all this show that the prisoner had not time that morning to do all the things that must have been done by the murderer? Taking it then that at a quarter past seven he left the house at that time there was no doubt he was seen by Bowles. Here? Coming from behind the house, sneaking out in an improper way? No, coming out of the gate where he ought to come if he was an innocent man. Bowles said he stated he was going turnipping, and he might have thought of doing so in the afternoon. Then they went with him to Salcot. He was seen passing the woolve by Foakes, who had been sentenced to three months imprisonment for killing a hare, and another time fined £2; and he was not aware that there was any rule of etiquette that compelled this young man to speak to a companion he did not like, and who might have been out poaching the night before. Yet the trifle was made the most of.

"To the jealous mind, trifle light as air

Are confirmations strong as holy writ;"

but only to the jealous. The inference was, that at that time, he had placed the razor under the woolve; unfortunately for this young man he was seen passing the woolve, and therefore he must have put the razor underneath. Did they see their way clearly to that? Could he have done so? The person must have gone out of his way who did it. Those who conducted this prosecution would have done well had they compared the foot-marks; they would have done their duty much better had they done this --- they ought to have done it, having the whole of the machinery of justice at their command; and because they had not done their duty, were they to supply the omission. As to the handkerchief, his sister said he had one similar to that found, this sister found it in her drawers. Alluding to the money, he asked if the prisoner were conscious that the half-crowns were those he took from the till in Cobb's room, would he have gone to Salcot, after the news of the murder was spread abroad, and then changed one of them. If so the prisoner must be the very incarnation of guilt. Next came the trowsers, and the blood thereon; in some cases, persons when charged with crimes, knowing that were guilty, would tell falsehood respecting such marks, and their statement would be proved to be false; but here there was a reasonable answer to the spots, and that made at once, which he (Mr. Parry) submitted was conclusively favourable to him; and his sister swore that he had been pig killing. It was impossible the blood could have got upon the prisoner, and Dr. Taylor says it would fly in a contrary direction, and with all his experience Dr. Taylor said he could not account for the blood upon his trowsers. Then another extraordinary part of this case was his falling down the sea wall, while with a witness for the prosecution. According to the tenor of the evidence, the blood might have been upon the clothes for a long time --- not one breathed a word about the recent appearance of the blood. There was no time for the prisoner to put the ink upon them on the day he was apprehended, as he was in the company of Emery all day. Then with respect to rubbing, did not the man fall; and how on earth could he get the mud off without rubbing? They remembered Mr. Codd's evidence, which was highly creditable to him, for he told the prisoner at the inquest "you are suspected, and will you give evidence." The reply was, "If you please, Sir."

"No," said Mr. Codd, "it is as you please --- you are a suspected party, and will you give evidence?" He then volunteered, and Mr. Codd said he gave it in clear straightforward manner. His manner had about it all the demeanour and elements of innocence; and through the whole of his conduct from morning to evening from one point of time to the other, was there anything at all in his conduct that led to a presumption of guilt? The old style of the law was thus --- is he guilty or not guilty, and did he fly for it – that is, did he go out of his place of abode and try to get away from others, and do anything that showed a consciousness of guilt. If they had seen him flying from others and baffling the efforts of those who were after him, they would have said, that is proof of guilt – his own conduct shows it and we cannot listen to argument or eloquence, however powerful, we must be guided by our own instinct and common sense; he was haunted by the guilt he had perpetrated and was ashamed to stop where he was. But if flying from justice was a proof of guilt, let him beg of them to remember that a man going about his calling in a quiet way was evidence of his innocence. Then he was examined, and they would find that substantially there was not a word of untruth in his statement. Now let him come to his conduct at Wivenhoe. Was his saying, "I wish to get a place on board ship instead of working on the land for 16d. a day," to be taken as evidence that he had committed the murder? That would not be tenable for a moment. Then he was reported to have said, "I cannot think how the woman could have been murdered, with the child lying, as it was, in the crib two feet off;" but if he heard of the murder, as he was likely to have done, this was an observation that would strike the mind of everybody; and that he had heard of it was probable, for news of this kind flew like electricity. These, said he are the facts of the case. The sense of responsibility with which I began is not diminished in going through the evidence. I do feel there are some extraordinary facts that take it out of the course of cases of this kind, when supported by consecutive and uncontradicted circumstantial evidence, at almost every step you find something favourable to the prisoner --- something extraordinary; so extraordinary as to prevent the possibility of inferring that he is the guilty man. That sense of responsibility has not been weakened by my considering the whole of this case. None but He who rules us all knows who committed that murder --- this man may be innocent, and for want of ability may have failed to press the points in his favour on your minds with sufficient power, but do not forget that this is only suspicion, and suspicion is not guilt; and let me not be understood as meaning that he is entirely innocent, which no human being can say, but that it is not proved before you, and will you be parties to taking the life of a human being, unless on clear and satisfactory evidence. Remember your verdict is irremediable. If once you pronounce a verdict of guilty, we shall have in this country that disgusting and brutalizing spectacle of the image of God being strangled by the common hangman and this human being, now before you, full of life and health like yourselves, will be committed to the scaffold. Remember your verdict is irremediable. It is the only verdict a jury has to pronounce in which after sentence is executed there is no remedy. Once the life of that man is exterminated, there is no remedy[23]. If transportation is inflicted on an innocent man, tardy remission may be made; but here, if you pronounce that verdict, his doom is fixed, and the scaffold is his end. I entreat of you, as you expect mercy to be merciful; and I hope it may not be met with a sneer, it I say humbly in the presence of his Lordship, and in the presence of a still higher power. I pray God to direct you to a right verdict.

His Lordship commenced his summing up, by observing that they would have to say whether the evidence brought against the prisoner forced them to the conclusion that he was the murderer. He explained to them the nature of circumstantial evidence, and also that

---

[23] There was no process of appeals at this time

of direct testimony, noticing the objections and suspicions to be attached to either. Some facts were perfectly clear; that the unfortunate woman was murdered that morning, about the time alleged by the prosecution was plain; that a robbery was also effected was clear, and that would be the motive for the murder. They would go with him thus far; but then it was for them to consider who the murderer was. If the hammer was the implement used, the prisoner was not contacted with it. The prosecution alleged the hammer was the instrument, but it was for them to consider whether it was the hedge stake, the hammer, or some other article; the prisoner was said to have been near the house, so were other people, for there were many cottages around, but they were called to prove they had left their houses for work before the time of the murder. The half-crowns were a most material part of the case, as it was suggested that they were stolen out of Mason's box; and if it could have been proved that his mother had given them to him, it would have been in his favour, but she was not called. Where a crime was so awful, and traced by direct testimony, they wanted no evidence of motive of the person committing such an offence, but the motive was always very material in a case of circumstantial evidence. The prosecution said the motive of the prisoner to commit the murder was, plunder; and there was no doubt that the man who did commit the robbery committed the murder also; and as there was no proof that the prisoner had any vindictive feelings towards the murdered woman, it could only be the discovery of the robbery. But it was said his motive was to obtain money, and they would see what was said by the witness Pudney, which was a very material matter for their consideration --- that evidence was very material in this case. The observation the prisoner made to that witness, was a most remarkable one, and if they believed him, it was against the prisoner. People were very apt to make a slight difference in reporting a conversation; and this witness had been twice in trouble for poaching, and it was represented to them in the able speech of the learned counsel for the defence, that this witness might possibly take advantage of the unhappy occurrence, to make a holiday, knowing that he would be paid by the prosecution; but it was for the jury to say what reliance they could place upon this witness, and they would judge how far that observation of the prisoner induced them to place reliance upon the evidence for the prosecution. He did not lay much stress upon what the prisoner said about his going to sea; that was an expression of as reckless man, who did not care about work, and who wanted to get out of the country. It was not at all inconsistent with the prisoner's guilt that he should have conducted himself as he had done, because a man who would commit such a crime would brave it out by his own wicked demeanour; but on the other hand, no doubt his conduct except one particular part, where it was suggested that he endeavoured to escape the observation of the man Foakes who met him upon the footpath --- with the exception, there was nothing, so far as appearances went, that was inconsistent with the conduct of a perfectly innocent man. Well, the next important fact in this case was, the circumstances of the blood marks discovered upon him at Salcot, --- that they were spots of blood there could be no doubt, in his endeavouring to efface that blood by ink was a most strong fact in this case of circumstantial evidence. These spots must have been put on in the course of the day --- after seven o'clock in the morning, and it was not proved that he did not use ink during the day, as he might have had access to some in the different public houses he called at. Probably they would come to the conclusion these were blood spots. Whether the ink was put there to efface them, would be for them to consider; --- what they would infer he could not say, but it must have been put on to efface that which the prisoner did not wish to have discovered. All he could say in favour of the prisoner was, that from suspicion being entertained that he was the murderer, and supposing he were innocent, he might by possibility, like a foolish man, have thought is wise in him to efface the marks of blood; it was extremely foolish and ridiculous; it might possibly be the conduct of an innocent man, but if so, certainly most folios. In going through the evidence, he would point out such observations as might occur to him. It seemed impossible to deny that suspicion was attached to the prisoner, but they would recollect that suspicion was not enough --- not even great suspicion on their part --- but that they must have a moral conviction --- that was all that could be required. They must ask themselves whether, these circumstances considered altogether, if they were substantiated before them as facts, led them, to the exclusion of all moral doubt, to think that the prisoner, on the morning in question, entered the house and committed the robbery and murder; they must take them into their consideration, --- it must be their verdict; --- they must consider his observations just so much as they thought they were intrinsically worth, and no more.

His Lordship then went through the whole of the evidence, and in alluding to the footmarks seen near the woolve by the witness Foakes, he observed that they most certainly ought to have been compared because if they agreed with the prisoner's shoe, it would have been a strong fact against the prisoner; and if they did not correspond, it would have been a very cogent circumstance in his favour. After recapitulating the voluminous mass of testimony adduced by the prosecution, the learned Judge concluded as follows: --- It may be only a strong case of suspicion against the prisoner, and a man must not be convicted on suspicion; if you have no moral doubt of his guilt --- if you cannot conscientiously and honestly come to any other conclusion, than for the purpose of obtaining this money (and there is something that the prisoner wanted some,) he committed the robbery and murdered the unfortunate woman; --- if all the circumstance of this case lead your mind to the conclusion that the prisoner at the bar is guilty, it will be your duty to convict him, whatever may be the consequences that follow; but, on the other hand, if after giving your best attention to all the facts, your minds are not brought to a moral conviction that the prisoner is guilty, it will be your pleasing duty to acquit him; and whatever your duty is, I am sure you will do it.

About seven o'clock the jury retired and at five minutes to nine returned into court with a verdict of NOT GUILTY.

Shortly after the verdict was given, his Lordship said he would not allow John Wash, and Mary, his wife, their expenses.

6 Conclusions

To summarise the inquest and the court case, it appears that Henry Harrington almost immediately became the chief suspect in the case, but it also turned out that this suspicion was based entirely on circumstantial evidence. Before the inquest, Harrington was quickly suspected, this, after an initial suspicion that fell upon the husband of Elizabeth Cobb fell through due to witnesses for Cobb. The fact that James Cobb was proved to have left the house at around about 6.30am, just after Mason had left the house. He had arrived at his boat around 7 o'clock and went about his work.

The main reasons for suspecting Harrington in the first place, seemed to be based on his look, it being mistrustful and him being of bad character. It was that characteristic that had Fox, the Night Constable, seek out Harrington for questioning, followed by his arrest by another village Constable, Beckwith and his return to Tollesbury to face an inquest as the chief suspect. Harrington did not resist and told the inquest he would answer any questions they had for him.

At the eventual trial, Harrington's defence made a point of informing the jury that Harrington had co-operated and had even consented to questioning by the Coroner's inquest and that it was voluntarily on Harrington's part. He was to be treated as innocent until proven guilty, although there was a fair-sized influence to the opposite given the reports of the inquest. The burden of proof was on the prosecution to convince the jury that Harrington was guilty, but given the circumstantial nature of the evidence, that was to prove too difficult for them.

At the inquest though, the discovery of a hammer, from Wash's house, with a head that seemed to fit one of the victim's head wounds, gave impetus to a village, shocked to the core, and looking for retribution, to immediately choose who they thought was most likely to have committed the crime. The pressure seemed too great for the authorities, who immediately arrested Harrington on suspicion of wilful murder, and charged him soon after his arrest.

The initial scientific investigation at the site of the murder was flawed in as much as the doctors both missed the more detailed aspects of the wounds having been caused by several blows to the head, given the observation on post-mortem, the fracturing of the skull in several places. That last fact was only discovered on this much more detailed investigation.

Even the evidence that Harrington needed money to secure his boat from Wivenhoe, was flawed. This was not assisted by the prosecution finding a witness who swore he had discussed getting money with Harrington and that the latter had said that Harrington knew where some money was, and that Harrington was determined to get it. It was damning evidence, albeit still circumstantial, if it had been interpreted by the jury as meaning that Harrington was going to obtain that money by illegal means, such as robbery. The witness though, turned out to be someone extremely unreliable and looking for a holiday in Chelmsford and was also expecting to be paid for his 'efforts' to be there.

The finding of the hedge stake on the Saturday following the murder, did Harrington no favours either in the eyes of a village that had already mentally committed him to death. It was the enterprising nature of Constable Fox, who was the first person to search the garden area of Cobb's cottage. It might have been searched much earlier than that, but no one seemed to want to do anything that might let Henry off from the charge of murder. Exactly why Fox went there on the Saturday, some four whole days after the event, is never to be known, but it may be that his suspicion was waning somewhat, after his interviews with the prisoner's sister, about his handkerchiefs, etc.

Fortuitous for Henry, the finding of a second viable weapon was going to prove vital, once detailed medical and scientific investigations were underway, including the discovery of multiple blows to the victim's head. Nevertheless, Harrington remained the chief suspect. There must have been several persons that did not wish for a second instrument to be brought forward, that would distract attention to the hammer they produced at the inquest. Luckily the hedge stake was also produced, and despite being side-lined by the doctors, remained a possible weapon at the trial several months later. Professional jealousy may have prevented the doctors from retracting their initial evidence that the stake was not powerful enough, we will never know, but the practise of allowing two different initial investigations to go ahead, may have caused more harm than good to the prosecution.

His Lordship's summing up covered the evidence as discussed above, together with the blood stains and the ink spots. He pointed out that suspicion alone was not enough to convict someone of a crime, but if the jury thought he had done it then guilty was to be their only verdict. As it was, the jury returned a verdict of Not Guilty and Henry Harrington walked out a free man again.

All in all, I believe Henry Harrington was an innocent man, or at least, it could not be proved that he had definitely murdered Elizabeth Cobb. He had no proven grievance with the woman or her family. He went about his work as usual that day, except that he 'went missing' according to some villagers, but only because he was destined to travel to Wivenhoe, with his friend, to see the boat that he was prepared to purchase with his collective monies. The fact that he had money, greater than that he had earned pulling turnips, was a major part of the suspicions that arose around him. The trip, a fair walk from Tollesbury to Wivenhoe, kept him out of the village all day and night and his visit was well known.

It is worth discussing these 'trips' by labourers, by today's standards, very arduous and time-consuming journeys on foot across open fields and footpaths. I have discovered some evidence of similar excursions by dredgermen, albeit some 25 years later. John Leather, in his book *The Salty Shore* (1979), recalls Tollesbury mariners, then involved in the yacht racing industry, walking the twelve miles to Wivenhoe, on the river Colne. They would start at 5 a.m. on a Monday and by 8 p.m. they would be on their yachts to start preparations for a week of racing, walking home again on the Friday[24]. So, it is within the bounds of possibility that Harrington and his friend, two young and fit labourers, walked that distance on the day of the murder, and then back as far as Salcot, to spend the night in that village.

Harrington had several events and witnesses against him. As his defence pointed out, the razor being found on the track between Tollesbury and Salcot, was the most damning and the jury may have been persuaded that was enough to convict him. However, in an atmosphere of caution regarding the sentencing of the guilty parties of capital offences, Harrington looks to be lucky that they did not do so.

The fact that he had secured money to buy a boat was another part of the evidence that may have provided the undoubted motive for the crime. His sister though, gave evidence that secured at least a doubt that the gain had been ill-gotten. I think this money was the major part of the villager's suspicion surrounding Harrington. It does not take much convincing of fellow villagers that the money had been stolen from the house, and who else had excess monies that day, but Harrington.

This feeling and keenness to convince themselves and of course the Coroner, that Harrington was the murderer is somewhat disturbing, but there is evidence to suggest the motive behind the villager's conviction (pun not intended). Harrington was described by one of the newspaper articles as being of 'bad character'.[25] Another paper, gave a description of the prisoner thus:

'He is of thick, sturdy build, rather short in stature, of dark complexion, and of a resolute or dogged cast of countenance'[26].

---

[24] John Leather, *The Salty Shore* (Seafarer Books, Woodbridge 2003) p. 186

[25] *Essex Standard*, Friday 05 December 1851

[26] *London Daily News*, Wednesday 03 December 1851

This description may suggest a brave looking, yet of a malicious appearance, at least to the newspaper reporter that had covered the inquest. It may have meant nothing of course, but it was clear that some of the villagers mistrusted Harrington enough to accuse him of wilful murder.

When Henry is researched via the historical records, it becomes obvious that he was an outsider to the village. He was not born and raised in Tollesbury, unlike the victim, her husband and Mr Wash, all of which were Tollesbury people from birth, according to the records. Henry, and his sister Mary, were not of the village. Henry was born in nearby Salcot and his sister was of White Colne, much further north towards Colchester, although both were brought up in Salcot, the father being the local baker.

> 'We must not listen to the desperate or the furious; but it is therefore necessary for us to distinguish who are the really indignant, and the really intemperate',

stated the philosopher Edmund Burke in his text *Maxims and Opinions, moral, political and economical* (1804)[27]. Burke understood discontent, one that had emerged from a new wave of liberalism and particularly of individualism. These 'virtues' had grown through the mid-Victorian period, long after Burke's intervention, yet it might explain how some of the Tollesbury villagers had come to form their opinions of Harrington as a murderer, despite the lack of real evidence.

In the face of a growing liberalism, how do simple village folk express themselves and make their opinions known? Basically, by ignoring the liberals and maintaining their views, however wild or intemperate they might appear. Of course, these same villagers are not overtly objecting to liberalism, they might not even know it exists as a concrete entity. By assuming guilt on this man, they do not trust, and one that appears to be of bad character, they convince themselves of his guilt, seemingly well before the inquest, let alone

---

[27] Edmund Burke, *Maxims and Opinions* (Whittingham, London 1804) p.116

the trial. This was not a new phenomenon. Assuming guilt was rife before English Law adopted the 'presumption of innocence', thought to have been introduced to English Law after the regular intervention of Sir William Garrow (1760 – 1840). This transformation occurred in his criminal trials at the Old Bailey in London, England during the late eighteenth century. His adversarial role as a robust cross-examiner of prosecutors, is widely documented, but our interest is restricted to this system being an essential part of the English legal system by the time of Harrington's trial.

During Harrington's trial, the defence made great play of this legal framework in his opening statement. ' In England fortunately for those who live here, it was left for the crown to show who was guilty' Parry states. He knows the prosecution are heavily reliant on circumstantial evidence, so he reinforces the notion of having the prosecution proving guilt. He is also aware that the villagers are bent on finding Harrington guilty, so he warns the Jury to be conscious of the legal system and to stick to the facts of the case. 'Suspicion, however strong, would not do' he had explained to the jury.

Harrington was released from Chelmsford prison, on Saturday 6th March 1852, as reported by the *Chelmsford Chronicle*, Friday 12th March 1852. There was a 'large body of people assembled at the gaol' it reports, and concerned for his safety, the crowd being quite agitated at his release, he was probably placed into the protection of his family by some side exit, although the report is not specific on this matter.

Shortly after Harrington's discharge, the *Essex Herald* published the following in the letters column, under the grand title:[28]

CAPITAL PUNISHMENT AND THE TOLLESBURY MUDER

To the Editor of the Essex Herald

Sir, --- Irishmen have permitted their feelings towards the criminal to supercede respect for justice. Such a principle will never, I hope, be prominent in the verdicts of English juries. Yet there is a rumour abroad that the recent acquittal of Harrington on a charge of murder arose in part from no sympathy with the crime indeed, but from a perhaps even more demoralizing sentiment --- antipathy to the law. The numerous challenges of jurymen are said to have originated in a desire to have such only sworn as were known to be adverse to capital punishments.

However, an unsworn advocate may desire so to consult the safety of his client, I will not believe that an Essex juryman would justify the selection by postponing the sanctity of an oath to the vagary of his private opinion. If summoned in a capital case, he might perhaps ask of the judge that he should be excused, on the ground of being disqualified, by his religious eccentricities, from returning a verdict according to the evidence. In no other way can he divest himself of his responsibility, except perhaps by incurring a penalty for non-attendance. If, notwithstanding such avowal, he is compelled to serve he will at least have candidly perjured himself.

Permit me to quote two or three passages --- not from the Old, but from the New Testament, in reference to the punishment of death, which may tend to remove scruples. If they seem to others as conclusive as to myself.

St. Paul, at the tribunal of Festus, refused not to do if he had committed anything worthy of death. He not only here gives no intimation of his disapproval of death as a punishment, but also in writing to the Roman Christians, he speaks of aims which are worthy of death.

---

[28] *Essex Herald*, Tuesday 23rd March 1852

St. Peter inflicts that penalty on Ananias and Sapphira;

Nor do I suppose that the Holy Ghost would have dictated to him a sentence which it would afterwards misbecome a Christian, though uninspired judge, to pronounce.

I am, Sir, your obedient servant.

L. B. R., March 19, 1852.   *JUSTITIA*

The report above also featured in the columns of the *Chelmsford Chronicle*, Friday, 26th March 1852.

It is not clear who L.B.R. was, but whoever he may have been, his letter makes it quite clear, his disgust in the jurymen, or rather the advocates choice of such, who he saw as being prejudiced against capital punishment, by way of 'the vagary of his private opinion'. The writer refers to the religious conviction of the jurymen and claims the notion had been discussed in circles 'abroad', that we can only guess at their nature and motivation. Did L.B.R. think the country was being seen as weak in its judicial system? Possibly, but the country had effective guidelines for jurors[29]. In 1845, Sir George Stephen published his *Juryman's Guide*[30]. In this, Stephens sets out the codes of conduct for being a juryman in England. Written for the 'class from which jurymen are usually taken', Stephen explains how jurymen ought to be 'conscientious and intelligent'.[31] If not, Stephen continues, the country's trial by jury system becomes 'worse than an empty boast'.

---

[29] Contemporary texts had also been published by Sir Richard Phillips in 1811 (*On the Rights and Duties of Juries*) and by Thomas H Cornish (*The Juryman's Legal Handbook and Manual of Common Law*)

[30] Sir George Stephen, *Juryman's Guide* (Charles Knight & Co. 1845)

[31] Stephen, p. iv

Stephen stated that on the subject of 'evidence of circumstances' there were important rules to be observed[32]. Firstly, 'every fact must be accurately proved and every probable explanation, but one could be excluded. If the circumstances, however suspicious, allowed of a simple explanation involving no guilt, then a guilty verdict could not be declared in court. In Harrington's case, his brief had not exactly explained that it was a case where explanations could be made not involving Harrington being the murderer, but he must have put doubt in the minds of the jurymen for them to return a verdict of Not Guilty, irrespective of their religious leaning, and based exclusively on Stephen's or other established 'rules'.

---

[32] Stephen p. 38

8 After the Trial

The *Herts Guardian, Agricultural Journal* ran a small report on the 3rd April 1852, shortly after the acquittal[33]. There had been 'popular dissatisfaction' in the village after the trial, with the verdict, it read. They reported that some of the villagers had held a mock trial in the village square. Another newspaper reported on the same event. The *Suffolk Chronicle* on 20th March 1852, reported the event, but with further information regarding this mock trial.

Its stated that an effigy representing Harrington had been made and that day was drawn in a cart through the parishes of Salcot, Tollshunt D'Arcy and Tollesbury. It drew into the village an immense crowd, estimated to be between 1500 and 2000 people. A large platform had been erected in Tollesbury square, not a stone's throw from where Elizabeth Cobb had been murdered. A number of tea chests had been placed upon the platform. Seated on each in full costume, were villagers as the officials of the court of justice, both fishermen and labourers taking part in the enactment. The mock ceremonials of the trial being completed in a most exciting manner by those engaged in it, and the jury having returned a verdict of guilty upon the effigy of Harrington, together with effigies of two of the witnesses that had 'displeased' the villagers at the real trial (unnamed), the whole structure was set alight and reduced to ashes[34].

There had also been a firing of a large quantity of gunpowder to accompany the proceedings, together with 'hootings and yells, groans and imprecations of an indignant and excited populace', the report stated. Although this act of mob justice was of great interest, it had been performed in comparative order, without the commission of

---

[33] *Herts Guardian, Agricultural Journal*, 3rd April 1952

[34] These effigies were probably of John and Mary wash, Harrington's sister and brother-in-law.

any damage, or any breach of the peace. Everyone retired to their homes at about 9 o'clock in the evening.

This show of determined disquiet, although carried out orderly, was in effect a protest at the justice system, rather than anything rebellious. Such mock trials had been recorded before 1852. They had ancient foundations according to Iain Mcalman, in his text *Radical Underworld: Prophets, Revolutionaries and Pornographers in London 1795 - 1840* (1988). These were socially irreverent popular customs practiced by rural recreational groups and urban fraternities such as trade and apprentice clubs, etc. They 'served various purposes, the most obvious being to undercut traditional authority by ridiculing its roles, functions and symbols of distinction' he argues[35]. Thus, no serious harm was meant in the Tollesbury event, but it probably resulted in an unburdening of some pent-up frustration with the outcome of the trial. Even so, it might have been an embarrassing time for the Wash's that lived so close to the village square. Their failure to commit recognition to the razor, being the obvious challenge to the villagers.

There are no further reports of this or any other demonstration. Tollesbury returned to being a quiet yet prospering fishing village. By the late Victorian era it became a centre of excellence for yacht racing, some of its inhabitants being chosen to race in the America Cup races of the day and by 1904 Tollesbury had a rail link that served as a fast connection for the products of its fishing industry together with a thriving salt production company.

---

[35] Iain Mcalman, *Radical Underworld: Prophets, Revolutionaries and Pornographers in London 1795 - 1840* (Cambridge University Press, 1988)

9 The Fate of Henry Harrington, Innocent Man?

Based on the contents of a single newspaper report dated Saturday 22nd May 1852 it probably went something like this[36]:

Ever since his liberation, Henry could not stop feeling elated. His incarceration in Chelmsford gaol had taken its toll on his health. It had been a torrid time, even in the newly constructed cell, one of the 239 arranged each side of a corridor over three levels. The only relief Henry had looked forward to was his two hours a day exercise in the small airing yard within the prison walls.

He had been released just a day, when he found out that the villagers were to hold a mock court. He had not heard of such things, but after talking to his sister and brother in law, he decided that it was not safe to hang around in Tollesbury, but instead he went to Salcot to seek refuge with his family. This relief was short lived, since just a day after he arrived in Salcot he learnt that a procession was coming down the road past his family's bakery. He left by the back entrance and went across the fields towards Wigborough.

Feeling completely depressed at his rejection, he spent the next few weeks sleeping rough at the side to the footpaths and roads, keeping himself out of sight, especially during daylight hours. One morning, about 9 o'clock, he emerged from under a bush, which he had sought out the previous evening. Sitting up, he had not seen the man that was coming towards him from behind. When he finally saw him, it was too late for Henry to conceal himself again.

"Hello there, it's Henry isn't it, Henry Harrington?" called the man from across the road. He had stopped and turned towards Henry, who was still sitting on the grass verge. Henry twisted himself to face

---

[36] *Hampshire Chronicle*, Saturday 22nd May 1852

the man and instantly recognised him as one of his labourer friends from Wigborough.

"Hello Stanley, how are you?" said Henry. "I'm fine Henry, it's you I would be more worried about. I heard about your court case and was glad to see you get off", replied Stanley, coming over the road and sitting down next to him.

"I'm ok, getting by as usual" said Henry, 'these have been difficult days for me and the family.'

"Hmmm, not so sure about that Henry, you look as though you haven't eaten for weeks" said Stanley. Henry started to get up, but his legs were so weak now he could not stand without assistance. Stanley caught his arm and stood him up. He noticed how much his frame had been reduced to almost a skeleton.

"No, you're right Stan, if I could I would shoot myself if I could only manage it. If you know of any farmer with a gun, then bring him here to do that for me." Henry pleaded.

Stanley, thinking that it was not right to see anyone reduced to such a state of deprivation, decided to take Henry to his place for some food and to see what could be done for him. It was clear he could not look after himself, and Stanley took it upon himself to see if the local union would take Henry in. They walked slowly off to Stanley's cottage, some mile or two towards Wigborough. At Stanley's cottage, henry had a meal and then slept the rest of the day. In the evening Stanley went to see the local trustee for the Lexden and Winstree Poor Law Union at Stanway. When he arrived back henry was sitting up.

'There you are Stanley,' he said, 'I was wondering just where you had got to.'

'I went to see the Union Trustee Henry and he said if you go along to Stanway they will find a place for you.' replied Stanley. Henry remained silent. 'For tonight though you are welcome to stay over.'

In the morning Henry gathered his things and left Wigborough via Abberton and made his way to Stanway.

That may have been the last that Stanley ever saw Henry. Henry certainly disappeared. That one newspaper report of the last sighting of Henry Harrington is all that hints at his destiny and the events around the Tollesbury murder. Maybe he left the Poor Union and got his place at sea. The records of Lexden Workhouse are incomplete for the period and today even his death remains a mystery.

His sister Mary, together with John Wash had three children and remained in Tollesbury till their deaths, at 83 and 68 respectively. As for James Cobb, Widower, he remained in Tollesbury and remarried another Elizabeth, but there does not appear to be any children from that marriage either.

Appendix I Census, Parish, Index and other Records

The following records concern the main Tollesbury protagonists involved in this case.

Henry Harrington:

First Name	Henry
Last name	Harrington
Birth/Baptism year	1831
Baptism date	01 May 1831
Birth Place	Salcot, Essex
Denomination	Anglican
Residence in 1851	96 East Street, Tollesbury
Church Description	St Mary the Virgin
Place	Salcot cum Virley
Father's first name(s)	Isaac
Father's occupation	Baker
Mother's first name(s)	Mary
Married at	Unknown
Death Record	Unknown

Elizabeth Cobb

First Name	Elizabeth
Last name	Cobb
Birth/Baptism year	1820
Baptism date	Unknown
Birth Place	Tollesbury, Essex
Denomination	Anglican
Residence (1851)	97 East Street, Tollesbury
Dedication	Anglican
Father's first name(s)	Isaac
Father's occupation	Baker
Mother's first name(s)	Mary
Married at	Unknown
Death Record	Maldon, 4a, 108
Place of Death	Tollesbury, Essex
Age at Death	33

James Cobb

First Name	James
Last name	Cobb
Birth/Baptism year	1815
Baptism date	Unknown
Birth Place	Tollesbury, Essex
Denomination	Anglican
Residence (1851)	**97 East Street, Tollesbury**
Church Description	St Mary
Father's first name(s)	Unknown
Father's occupation	Unknown
Mother's first name(s)	Unknown
Married at	Unknown and remarried
Death Record (79)	Maldon, 4a, 288 (or 233?) 1893
Place of Death	Tollesbury, Essex
Age at Death	79

Elisa Spurgeon:

First Name	Elisa
Last name	Spurgin (possibly Spurgeon)
Birth/Baptism year	1846
Baptism date	Unknown
Birth Place	Tollesbury, Essex
Denomination	Unknown
Residence (1851)	97 East Street, Tollesbury
Church Description	Unknown
Father's first name(s)	Unknown
Father's occupation	Unknown
Mother's first name(s)	Unknown
Married at	Unknown
Death Record (79)	Unknown
Place of Death	Unknown
Age at Death	Unknown

Mary Wash

First Name	Mary
Last name	Wash (nee Harrington)
Birth/Baptism year	1814 or 1816
Baptism date	Unknown
Birth Place	White Colne or Salcot, Essex
Denomination	Unknown
Residence (1851)	96, East Street, Tollesbury, Essex
Church Description	Unknown
Father's first name(s)	Isaac
Father's occupation	Baker
Mother's first name(s)	Mary
Married at	Unknown (probably Tollesbury)
Death Record (79)	Maldon, 3rd, 1899, 4a, 437,
Place of Death	Tollesbury
Age at Death	83 or 85

John Wash

First Name	John
Last name	Wash
Birth/Baptism year	1812 or 1813
Baptism date	Unknown
Birth Place	Tollesbury
Denomination	Unknown
Residence in 1851	96, East Street, Tollesbury, Essex
Church Description	Unknown
Father's first name(s)	Unknown
Father's occupation	Unknown
Mother's first name(s)	Unknown
Married at	Unknown
Death Record (79)	Maldon, 4th, 4a, 196
Place of Death	Probably Tollesbury
Age at Death	68